Hate Crime in India

G. S. Bajpai • Garima Pal
Tusha Singh • Advait Tambe

Hate Crime in India

Understanding Nuanced Discrimination Against North-Eastern Population

Springer

G. S. Bajpai
National Law University, Delhi
New Delhi, New Delhi, India

Tusha Singh
Faculty of Law
University of Delhi
New Delhi, India

Garima Pal
Maharashtra National Law
University Mumbai
Mumbai, Maharashtra, India

Advait Tambe
New York University School of Law
New York, NY, USA

ISBN 978-3-031-30521-4 ISBN 978-3-031-30522-1 (eBook)
https://doi.org/10.1007/978-3-031-30522-1

This Springer imprint is published by the registered company Springer Nature Switzerland AG
The registered company address is: Gewerbestrasse 11, 6330 Cham, Switzerland

Preface

The initial impetus for writing a book based on the finding of empirical research in the area of hate crime against Northeast people residing in metro cities came from a general awareness of the way in which hate crime incidents were increasing. The actual motivation came not only from a real interest in this area but from the opportunity to conduct and participate in such empirical research.

Due to certain shortcomings like lack literature, empirical studies, no substantive legal provisions entailing the rights of the victims of hate crime, guidelines for the law enforcement agencies on how to deal or address the grievances of Northeast people, led us to research in this particular area.

This book is an attempt to gather the experiences and problems encountered by Northeast people residing in metro cities. Furthermore, it also captures their perspective toward the legal assistance and other safety measures provided. The book tries to capture the perspectives of both Northeast people and the general population, whether there was a need of new law for hate crime incidents. This is also an attempt to tap the role of law enforcement agencies, our community, culture, mass media, and their implications with regard to hate crime incidences against Northeast people. This book also covers a series of case studies to have an in-depth understanding of hate crime and its aftereffects on the victim while undergoing the research study.

Through this book, we have formulated certain suggestions based on the findings of the research study. This book could benefit the functionaries toward systematic assistance to the needs of Northeast people. Many such suggestions can be made functional, thus providing some protection and benefit to Northeast people residing in metro cities in India.

New Delhi, India — G. S. Bajpai
Mumbai, Maharashtra, India — Garima Pal
New Delhi, India — Tusha Singh
New York, NY, USA — Advait Tambe

Acknowledgment

This book *Hate Crime in India – Understanding Nuanced Discrimination Against North-Eastern Population* is based on a project sponsored by the Indian Council of Social Science Research (ICSSR). This book would have not been possible without the support of ICSSR and the grant sanctioned by them as well as the stakeholders, i.e., field investigators and interns.

This book is an outcome of the cumulative effort of a team that has been regularly working over the research study conducted over a period of two years. The tasks involved was quite tedious, specially the data collection which posed several challenges to the field staff. My acknowledgments are due to all who have extended support to this venture. At the outset, I extend my sincere thanks and gratitude to ICSSR, for giving me and my team an opportunity to conduct this unique study covering six metro cities. I thank the target group (the Northeast people and the general population) who facilitated this research by patiently interacting with the research team and completed the questionnaires/interview schedules. I am also indebted to special police unit for Northeast people in Delhi for giving their insights over this issue. I would like to express my deepest appreciation to all those who provided me and my team the possibility to complete this study and develop it into a book. My thanks to the Project Consultant, Mr. Himanshu, whose contribution in stimulating suggestions and encouragement helped coordinate the project.

A special thanks goes to my research team Dr. Garima Pal, Ms. Tusha Singh, and Mr. Advait Tambe. Their dedication to the study ensured its successful completion. I have to appreciate the guidance given by the panels during our project presentations that has improved our skills, courtesy their comments and advice. Last but not the least, I also express my cordial thanks to the field investigators and the interns Ms. Athira Nair and Ms. Triya Ghosh. The study could not have been completed without the assistance and commitment provided by them.

National Law University, Delhi
New Delhi, New Delhi, India

G. S. Bajpai

Contents

Chapter 1
Introduction

India is known for its rich and diverse cultures and languages. For instance, the people of Northeast India practice very different customs and rituals, making it difficult for the mainland people to understand and accommodate Northeastern individuals who migrate to mainland India to seek better jobs or educational opportunities. In general, people from various places migrate to metropolitan cities for two main reasons, i.e., to have better employment opportunities and better education, which is highly prevalent among the Northeastern people. Unlike the mainland, Northeast India, primarily a tribal and hilly area without much development, attracts the people from Northeast to metro cities. When they arrive in metropolitan cities, they face many security issues at various places due to their appearance, making it easy to identify them as a person from the Northeast. This security threat is severe and permeates across interaction places such as educational institutions, workplaces, and dwelling places. It includes sexual harassment, racial discrimination, violence, and, in extreme cases, threats to life.

1.1 The Origin and Development of Hate Crime

The term "hate crime" seems to have been coined by journalists and policy advocates in the 1980s to describe a series of incidences of racial discrimination against African-Americans, Asians, and Jewish people (National Institute of Justice, n.d.). The term itself may seem new, but the incidence of hate crimes dates back to ancient civilizations; one example is the Roman Empire, which persecuted various religious groups. Some forms of hate crimes are extremely barbaric, the worst being Nazi Germany's persecution of the Jewish people during the Second World War. Other hate crime incidents that predate the terminological coining are slavery, caste discrimination, bonded labor, genocide, ethnic cleansing, etc.

G. S. Bajpai et al., *Hate Crime in India*,
https://doi.org/10.1007/978-3-031-30522-1_1

According to the Federal Bureau of Investigation (FBI), hate crime is defined as *"a criminal offence committed against a person, property, or society that is motivated, in whole or in part, by the offender's bias against a race, religion, disability, sexual orientation, or ethnicity/national origin."* It is thus evident from the above definition that a hate crime is not just committed against an individual but also the group which they represent, for instance, their race, religion, caste, gender, disability, sexual orientation, or ethnicity/national origin.

The Office for Democratic Institutions and Human Rights (ODIHR) in Europe also defines a hate crime as *"a criminal act committed with bias motives, that is, an offense motivated by intolerance towards a certain socially defined group, in that the "perpetrator intentionally chose the target of the crime because of some protected characteristics: race, religion, ethnicity, language or sexual orientation"* (OSCE – ODIHR, 2018).

1.1.1 International Perspectives on Hate Crimes

The concept of hate crime was first conceptualized and defined in the United States of America (USA), specifically concerning racial violence being committed against the African-American population of the country by white Americans. After the emancipation of the African-Americans in the USA, the former "slave class" strived to raise their standards of living and attain political power in American society. However, to date, racial discrimination and hatred against African-Americans continue to be committed by the white Americans as a display of their racial superiority. Today, hate crimes in the USA target African-Americans and various immigrants based on land of origin, skin color, language, religion, sexual orientation, etc. Gradually, every country in the world has started addressing this racial violence, discrimination, and any other kind of biased-motivated crimes under the umbrella of hate crimes. Still, the perspectives on these hate crimes remain varied from nation to nation.

In 1993, the racially motivated killing of Stephen Lawrence and the subsequent police investigation led to a drastic rise in recognition of crimes motivated by hate and prejudice in the United Kingdom (UK) (Chakraborti & Garland, 2012). The case, *R v Gary Dobson*, became significant and ignited the discussion for understanding the seriousness of hate crimes in the UK. Apart from racism, other grounds for hate crimes like religion, gender, and sexual orientation were also highlighted in the discussion, which led to the creation of hate crime legislation (Hurd, 2001). In the UK, during the late 1990s and early 2000s, many legal provisions were created concerning hate crime and protecting the victim's specific characteristics.

The Office for Democratic Institutions and Human Rights (ODIHR) is the institution of the Organization for Security and Cooperation in Europe (OSCE), an intergovernmental organization with 57 countries from Europe, Central Asia, and North America. The ODIHR is helping participating states comprehensively encounter hate crimes by bringing together government institutions, civil societies, criminal justice systems, and international organizations (OSCE – ODIHR, 2019). ODIHR also supports participating states in designing and developing monitoring mechanisms and data collection on hate crimes (OSCE – ODIHR, 2019). However, in 2017, only 39 out of 57 countries reported official hate crime data to ODIHR, including the disaggregated official hate crime statistics for 23 countries. This indicates a nonserious attitude of governments toward the grave nature of hate crimes and allied incidences.

1.1.2 Hate Crime in India

Racial hate crime is not unique to the USA and is witnessed in India, along with other hate crimes based on religion, caste, and gender. Hate crimes against Northeast Indians are quite prevalent, especially in metropolitan cities like Delhi, Pune, Mumbai, Bangalore, Hyderabad, and Chennai. The reasons motivating such hate crimes against Northeast Indians are umpteen and will be subsequently discussed in this book. Unfortunately, despite hate crimes drawing considerable attention from the public and the authorities, measures to prevent victimization are insufficient (Box 1.1).

Box 1.1: Examples of Hate Crime in India

For instance, on a December evening in Safdarjung, South Delhi, three young men from Manipur were buying vegetables from a vendor outside the entrance to their stairwell. When one of them started negotiating the price of the vegetables in Hindi, the vendor joked about their use of Hindi and said, "kaha kaha se chale aate hai." Northeast Indians at their offices in Gurugram were asked if they were from Bangkok or Thailand, and the Northeastern women were teased because of their physical appearance. Northeastern students at Delhi University face comments like "chinky," "momo," and "chowmien" regularly. One of the customers at the restaurant was overheard speculating with her companion about whether the Northeastern workers were migrant workers from China. Similar scenes are witnessed in Delhi, Bangalore, Mumbai, Pune, Chennai, and Hyderabad and are increasing daily as per the empirical data collected in further chapters.

Indians have always been proud of their culture and the old adage of unity in diversity. People from all backgrounds, races, castes, religions, gender, or sexual orientation from different corners of this vast topography have accepted its diversity. However, while studying the issue of hate crimes against Northeast Indians, it was seen that Indians view India as being divided into two parts – one which consists of those they view as citizens and another which is erroneously understood to be of the people from a different land. As a result, Northeastern Indians face social exclusion as they are perceived as foreigners rather than Indians – this can be seen from the case studies at the end of the chapters. Moreover, the seven sister states of the country are not distinctly known to a large section of India. Because of geographical unawareness and differences, a divide is created and furthered among the people of India. This divide is why hate crimes occur in the first place and invariably go unpunished. Through this book on "Hate Crimes on Northeast Indians," the authors studied the various reasons behind this divide, which could vary from geographical differences, physical features, or way of life, to name a few.

Northeast people are considered to be a backward section of our society. This is majorly because of multicultural disputes and terrorist activities that have taken place in the Northeastern region. It leaves a lesser scope of development for the area and its people. Hence, the people of the Northeastern region seek educational or employment opportunities from the metropolitan cities in the mainland. This makes the mainland residents averse to the Northeasterners who consider these so-called "foreign people" as encroachers to their lands. This is also the reason why they experience exclusionist behavior from mainland Indians. Furthermore, there is no doubt that the isolation of tribal people from the main community has led to the exploitation of tribal populations everywhere. This notion of abnormality, i.e., that the tribal are different from the "normal" populace, has led to their constant exploitation. The tribal people are deprived of fundamental rights otherwise guaranteed to any citizen of India for the sole reason of them being different, which is what happens to the Northeasterners. When they come in contact with the mainland inhabitants, they suffer through a differential treatment through stereotypes, racial slurs, remarks, and physical and sexual assaults, as per the case study analysis at the end of the chapters.

This creates tensions among communities, and acculturation further exacerbates the conflict between space and identity. The Northeast region is riddled with separatist and militant issues. Also, there has been a persistent viewpoint of feeling ignored and isolated among the Northeastern states. Thus, it becomes essential to raise the crucial issues regarding the perception and representation of the multiple ethnicities of the Northeast and its underlying narratives.

In the year 2014, the issue of prejudices and violence faced by people from Northeast India gained momentum when multiple cases of atrocities against them were brought to the limelight by the news and social media. Such incidents included various types of assaults, mostly of physical and sexual nature. However, many incidents still do not come to the forefront and are conveniently ignored by the mainstream public discourse. Apart from the incidents that result from the prejudices against Northeastern Indians, the COVID-19 pandemic has caused further bias and a rise in hate crimes against Northeastern Indians. This is because the Northeasterners are mistaken for the Chinese people and are treated discriminately. In this book on hate crimes, such events will be accounted for chronologically, along with a case study analysis of various incidents that came to light. The aim is to understand the trend of hate crimes committed against Northeast Indians.

After an in-depth study and analysis of cases, attempts were made to understand the general public's perspective toward Northeast Indians; this formed the central are to analyze the problem of hate crimes. Perception toward any group in society is what drives the people to act against them. Further, it is pertinent to note that what differentiates a hate crime from a conventional crime is the added perception or prejudice which becomes the main reason behind the commission of any hate crime against an individual. It is an indirect attack on the group or the community. Hate crime is unique as it is committed keeping in view the particular trait or characteristic of the victim. The feeling of vulnerability faced by the victims of such crimes is far worse than by victims of other crimes. These victims feel intimidated or threatened because it is an attack on such a characteristic of the victim, which is unchangeable. This makes the victim as well as the entire group vulnerable since the very objective of these types of crimes is to frighten the community as a whole.

Unfortunately, racial comments or name-calling have become a form of recognition for the Northeastern people in metropolitan cities and are a significant concern. These are verbal or digital hate crimes that are not included in the typical understanding of hate crimes. Furthermore, in cases where there is a physical injury, it is not considered "serious enough" by the authorities to take any action. This indifference is because of a lack of understanding of the hate crime. Even where the different incidences of hate came into the limelight, another issue emerged: the lack of specific legal provisions to curb such hate incidents.

Presently such hate crimes are dealt with in the Scheduled Castes and Tribes (Prevention of Atrocities) Act, 1989. However, the Act doesn't explicitly say anything about hate crimes against Northeast Indians, as most of the people hailing from the Northeast community belong to the Scheduled Caste (SC)/Scheduled Tribe (ST) category. This Act comes to their rescue, provided the victim specifically belongs to any of these categories. The Act doesn't recognize racial sets or legal provisions against racial discrimination toward Northeast people per se. Another provision that is invoked in such incidents is Section 153A of the Indian Penal Code, which might consider such acts provided the act/incident must promote hatred and ill will between communities on the grounds of race among others. The problem is that not all acts of racial discrimination necessarily incite hatred against different communities. The legal provisions superficially address the issue of racial discrimination, not hate crimes as a whole. Thus, as a reaction to an increase in hate incidence and lack of legal provisions, the Bezbaruah Committee was formulated, giving its recommendations to address this issue. The committee was a welcoming step with its own set of lacunas. The Committee captured the problem of the hate crimes faced by Northeast Indians. Instead of putting the acts against Northeast Indians under a hate crime, it devised a recommendation that catered to discrimination against the Northeastern Indian population. However, it failed to understand that discrimination is different from a hate crime because it involves an added prejudice against the victim community. The inherent "hate" drives the wrongdoer, unlike in cases of discrimination, which are mainly focused on the acts that the perpetrator has committed.

Hate crime is where an offense is committed against the victim with hate as motivation or the driving force. Discrimination is an objective way to look into this matter. This aspect is discussed in detail through this book along with the issues faced by Northeast Indians, focusing on other elements apart from the normative understanding of the hate crime incidences. These incidences are further explained in the case studies.

1.2 Literature Review

Northeast communities, groups, and individuals consider metro cities as one of the most unsafe places due to the upsurge in instances of racial and ethnic discrimination in recent times. Bias-motivated criminal acts, unlike other crimes, have specific characteristics. Perhaps that is the reason why hate crime is so peculiar in its nature and element. There are a few more pertinent questions to be answered, for instance, the lack of legal provisions, which has resulted in an insensitive attitude of people toward Northeast residents in metros.

For a clear and deep understanding, the authors applied a mixed approach, i.e., both doctrinal and empirical methodology to collect both qualitative and quantitative data. The authors further relied upon secondary data collected from available books and articles published and printed in the newspapers.

1.2.1 Hate Crime: Meaning, Policy, and Criminal Justice

There are about 420 different varied languages and dialects that are spoken in Northeast India. Hence, this region contains wide-ranging ethnos and diverse socio-linguistic configurations. "North-East Indians, the home of many Nationalities, is moving through different developmental and formational phase" (Samuel, 1993). This article effectively reflects the vital role of language in determining nationality and further elucidates other components of nationality formation. The author concluded that though language was just a vehicle for people to connect, it acted as an integral part of nationality.

The Nehruvian policy of noninterference with the cultural tradition and customs of tribal people was not that effective in catering to the linguistic and cultural development in the region. The authors have inferred that there was a clash of cultural aspirations with the idea of a new nation. Therefore, the formation of a new republic and unfulfillment of these aspirations lead to alienation and violence.

This consequent violation can take a very brutal form, better known as "hate crime." The term "hate crime" is very controversial with reference to its definition. Crimes motivated by intolerance toward certain groups in society are considered hate crimes. Such crimes have the inherent potential to divide communities and create a vicious cycle of violence and retaliation.

The author proficiently divided his article into three parts, making it quite simple to comprehend. The core of this article was the effect of federal and state-level statutes and the challenges the legal framework faces concerning hate crimes in particular (Murakami, 2004). However, the authors in this book are concerned only with hate crimes against Northeast Indians; the definitional part was for a better understanding of federal laws that govern the hate crimes in the USA.

Hate crimes are not an issue in our country alone but occur invariably in all countries around the globe. Therefore, it is imperative to have a stringent hate crime statute that eventually will deter such serious offences. This also sends a strong message to the offenders that a just and humane society wouldn't tolerate such behavior. Additionally, recognizing the harm done to victims would convey to individual victims and their communities the understanding that the criminal justice system serves to protect them (Reuter, 2009). Hence, this practical guide for prosecuting hate crimes by the UK took due care to ensure it remains relevant while applying it in different legal systems in the OSCE region.

Along similar lines, the UK guide to Prosecuting Hate Crimes (OSCE, 2014) further explored the development of defective policies of the government and criminal justice actors to ensure the successful prosecution of hate crimes. The guide, with utmost clarity, manifests the meaning and consequences of hate crimes and various policy implementations related to such crimes. It thoroughly discusses the process of building a prosecution case and provides the litmus test for recognizing the indicators that the case might be of hate crime. It also stipulated the key types of evidence and counter-defenses to prove the motive. The guide was drafted by legal experts yet in a comprehensive way in which people without legal expertise may comprehend it easily.

Further, the constitutional, international, and policymaking-related issues of hate crime had been discussed in detail in a book by Gernstenfeld (2011). However, the authors focus only on Indian aspects of hate crimes and the analysis in connection to the injustice and violence encountered by Northeast Indians residing in metro cities.

1.2.2 Origin of Hate Crime: Intolerance or Ignorance?

In the last few decades, hate crime instances have been referred to as a unique category of victimization and motivated bias. This study investigated the influence of social status on attributions of blame in specific instances of hate crimes. In his research, Lyons suggested that gay and lesbian victims were held more accountable for their actions than heterosexual victims and the respondent's attitude shaped attributions of blame. The stigma perspective meant that the public would deride minority status individuals, whereas the sympathy perspective implied that the public would be sympathetic to minorities (Lyons, 2006).

The article (Karukus & Goregenli, 2011) was very constructive as it helped the authors of this book draw additional insight into attitudes and beliefs, leading to tolerance or hostility toward the victims of hate crimes. It studied hate crimes in Turkey based on the relations between homophobic ideologies and the perception of liability of perpetrators and victims of hate crimes based on sexual orientation. The qualitative data collected from 281 university students using hate crime vignettes was quite beneficial. Therefore, the authors of this book adopted a similar approach to conduct the current study on hate crimes against Northeast Indians in metro cities.

1.2.3 The Mongoloid Race or Racism

There was a time when people extensively referred to Northeast Indians as people belonging to the Mongoloid race. However, the research team aimed to study and understand various forms of violence against Northeast people in India, which might have emerged due to racial differences.

An article (Baruah, 2008) described the abovementioned race as a social category resulting from practices. However, he stated that even if the race stopped being accepted as a social category, it didn't mean that human beings would stop making distinctions based on stereotypical phenotypes or skin color. The authors found this article very useful since it elucidated on a different dimension to hate crime – as it focused on the persistent political aspects of race in the Northeast. This book aims to study those offenses arising from racial discrimination and find the possible consequences of such crimes.

A critical introduction to race, racism, and criminal justice to provide an up-to-date and comment on what impact it had on cultural and racial politics in the UK was done (Hindpal Singh Bhui, 2009). However, as it mainly focused on refugees and asylum seekers as victims and their link between ethnicity and drug use, not much was captured by the team on the race. This book aims to understand various forms of violence against the Northeast people in India.

The legal guidelines and various safeguards in accordance with which these tribes are governed in India generally affect the nature of these tribes, as well as the protective measures and administrative guidelines for tribal protection and development (Thakur, 2009). Thakur's book was very resourceful to the authors, as the main focus was on safeguards and measures. But whether these can be enough to protect Northeast residents in metros remained an unanswered question. Therefore, the authors, through the findings formulated after the completion of their study, tried to gather opinions of the people of the Northeast residing in metro cities on the discussion mentioned above.

Indians residing in the mainland have a notion of how one should eat, behave, look, and dress. This generally leads to discrimination against the Northeast people due to their Mongolian phenotypes and different food and clothing habits. It has led to mainland Indians stereotyping Northeast Indians. However, the author commented that one way to fight it is by implementing laws to deal with such injustice (Hazarika, 2017). The authors agreed with what Hazarika had commented as it is useful to understand why the discrimination subsists. However, laws are not enough; we must go beyond the laws by influencing the most difficult and sensitive of tools: the human mind.

1.2.4 *Migration to Metro City: A Tricky Path*

The experiences gained from the past death of Richard Loitam and Dana Sangam identified the presence of racially discriminatory ideology in the people. However, it is ignored by the government and academicians (Thounaojam, 2012). The authors agree with Swar Thounaojam as the paper also highlighted the triad representation in which Northeast people were referred to like those for sportsperson, women, and entertainment. The reasons why the Northeast population migrated and why metro cities were chosen as a destination for this migrant population were discussed extensively in this writing, including various struggles they face regarding lifestyle, employment, education, and social inclusion.

Delhi is one of the most favored destinations of migrants from the Northeast, mainly for educational and employment purposes (Ramesh, 2012). Although Ramesh discussed various dimensions of the outmigration of youth from India's Northeastern region to Delhi, he was of the view that central to the hardships of the migrants in the city was a cultural gap between the migrant and local societies. Although the authors in this book were trying to understand the main reason behind prejudice against Northeast migrants, this article was beneficial as it comprehensively provided the required logical data for such discrimination and racial concerns.

The connection between borderlands and heartlands through migrants leaving Northeast regions and migrating to metro cities was analyzed by Duncan McDuie-Ra in his article (McDuie-Ra, 2013). Authors of this book in response to hate crimes in metros took a similar stance that racial inequality, ill-treatment, and discrimination persisted.

The inability to understand others' cultures led to huge disparity and misjudgment; often, it led to disrespect of someone's cultural practices that caused many undesired hostilities. For example, the experience of students from the Northeast who came to study and work in Delhi was subjected to various kinds of discrimination because of their different phenotypes and cultural habits; the article tried to understand the multiple problems of Northeast students in the city, because of their language barrier. Northeast India is one of the country's most diverse, culturally rich and environmentally healthy regions and is referred to as the land of multiple ethnicities. They are often considered far from mainland India, hence face the dilemma of being ignored and isolated. The referenced article raised issues regarding the perceptions and representation of the multiethnicity of the Northeast and analyzes the dilemma of the people of the region (Jain, 2016). This research paper helped the authors of this book understand how culturally rich these regions were and provided a broad perspective as to why there were cultural gaps between mainland people and Northeast.

1.2.5 The Problem of Multiculturalism

Description of Northeast India to the world is that it is a hotspot of ethnic violence, extremism, and insurgency. This region was seen as the rise of extremist organizations, challenging the sovereignty and integrity of the Indian states, and this also mobilized the people on ethnic lines. As per the author, social exclusion is a multidimensional term that encompasses the social, economic, and cultural spheres and comprises individual and group exclusion from society. It was usually related to the problem of equal opportunity (Bijukumar, 2013). This article also explained the concept of ethnicity, often identified with the ideas of primordialism based on race, kinship, history, language, etc. Northeast India is often regarded as the cultural mosaic of India, comprising diverse tribal communities, linguistics, and ethnic identities.

The sense of fear and exclusion started even before independence. This article explained the elite formation, the emergence of the middle class, politics over ethnicity, and ethnic conflicts.

The authors of this book agreed with Kumar that social exclusion and ethnicity reinforce each other in new contexts in Northeast India and that the main reason behind the violent conflicts is ethnicity. The authors have also relied on the concept by King and Leonard that focused on paradoxical relationships and repugnant reflection of social decay rooted in multiculturalism (Leonard, 2014).

1.2.6 The Perception of Mainland India

Various studies have shown that Northeast India often remains marginalized, stereotyped, and absent from the mainstream media. Due to a lack of attention to these regions, they have remained alien from mainland India. People from this region experience racism and discrimination in their own country, which the media have largely ignored. The negative representation of the Northeast region had created a negative image of this region in the minds of mainland people. Hence, the region remains underrepresented and misrepresented in the Indian mainland media (Raj, 2016).

This article focused mainly on underrepresentation, negative coverage, stereotyping, and reasons for such minorities in media. The author relied on various participants, including journalists, students, activists, teachers, and corporate lawyers. This underrepresentation led to alienation; it initiated a widespread belief among the Northeastern masses since it appeared not to be in the national interest and thus were not reporting in the Northeast. There was also a risk of threat to life in reporting due to the instances of bomb blasts and frequent instances of insurgency. Hence, media reporters hardly cover Northeast nor accord adequate footage during primetime.

Why do Northeast Indians have fewer options other than sports, insurgency, or migration? This question was addressed in the article (McDuie-Ra, 2016). The article was presented in six sections. The first section provided background on the Northeast and Manipur. The second described the concept of race in contemporary India; the third provided an analysis of the formation of the famous figure of Mary Kom at the national level. The fourth discussed crisis in race relations in India from 2012 onward, illustrated by the exodus of Northeast migrants from metro cities. Finally, the two figures showed a symbolic analogy, where Irom Sharmila was considered a counterpoint to Mary Kom. One evokes India's shame and the other Indian pride through this article.

The analysis of Central and State legal developments and enactments against bias-motivated crime is relatively underdeveloped. Furthermore, the complex dynamics between legislature and people advocating for their rights has led to this area of law being scantly researched (Wolfe, 2014). The analytical data showed Northeast as exotic, backward, anti-national, loose, and immoral, providing for discrimination and harassment and violence (McDuie-Ra, 2012). This book was one of the essential pieces of literature for studying hate crimes in Delhi. This book helped the authors in their in-depth study of the objectives of this book on hate crime. The authors also relied on the article by Kamei Samson (2017); this article provided insights into the formation, evolution, and consequences of racial divisions in Indian society, which the author didn't include.

1.2.7 The Committees and Recommendations

The death of Nido Tania evoked a nationwide stir. The Bezbaruah Committee was set up to investigate this issue in February 2014. The mandate was to listen to the issues raised by people from Northeast India living in metro cities. The Committee suggested measures that the government of India could implement. The authors found this report very helpful in formulating a comment stating the working and functioning of the judiciary and government regarding their concern toward this geographically isolated region (Bezbaruah, 2014).

The Law Commission's Report on Hate Speech, 2017 (Chauhan, 2017), was also noteworthy. The Commission recommended that the effect of any harmful speech made against the vulnerable group constituted discrimination and violation of their rights. They further proposed amendments in IPC by inserting new sections after Sections 153B and 505A. The authors fruitfully utilized these recommendations concerning hate crimes forming racial slurs against Northeast Indians. Therefore, this research study might prove to be very useful in the near future and could help locate measures to safeguard the interest of the Northeast people.

In her article, senior editor Lekshmi Priya S said that using derogatory words like *Chinki, Chinese, or Nepali* to these Northeast people was widespread. She found it was time that we stop claiming that racism does not exist in our country. As per her, mainland Indians had a bad habit of interfering in the matters of others (western countries), condemning them for racism, and conveniently choosing to ignore the same attitude directed to our fellow citizens.

Discrimination is no unknown word for us, any unjust behavior or attitude based on prejudicial treatment. When talking about Northeast, from the very beginning, this region has remained isolated from the so-called mainstream Indian culture. And it holds to be the exact reason for the existence of the prevailing discrimination, racism, and prejudices, from calling them chinky, Chinese, to Bahadur. The murder of Nido Tania was also a result of his retaliation toward the people mocking him for his facial expression, his looks, and the place he belonged. How Nido Tania died reflected the inefficiency of the authority in dealing with the case of Nido and how racial hatred led to his killing. Likewise, the case of the 26-year-old Manipuri girl who was assaulted, molested, kicked, and dragged by her hair in public, and no one came to her rescue. The list doesn't stop here. Discrimination not only exists in the contemporary world but has prevailed since independence, from Jawaharlal Nehru's times, when the Chinese invaded 50 years back. Here, the author emphasized the statistic of migrants from the Northeast region. Thus, it helped the research team understand law enforcement agencies' role. However, the author didn't cover what measures should be taken to protect the rights of the Northeastern people. Our study thus covered this area.

1.2.8 Changing Times: Changing Mindsets Curb Hate Crimes

Nevertheless, the government and judiciary had taken a few steps to protect Northeast Indians against the prevailing discrimination and racism (Barkataki, 2017). Bartaki here discussed the actions taken by the Supreme Court, stating not to let go of matters of racial abuse and discrimination against Northeast Indians. The authors completely agreed with Bartaki that setting up special cells for the protection of the Northeast Indians would be more problematic as it separated the people of the Northeast and its representation as one single entity. Instead of having northeast cells, it could be better to have an anti-discriminatory cell which would cover a broad range of issues and not detach the northeast people. It is to be noted that not only the government or the law could create amendments to the conditions of the region, but also the people could make a difference by changing their mindsets. The people could develop an overall thought process and provide a broader view of the Northeast region.

Punishing a person without authority or extrajudicial killing by a group, constituting mob lynching, is partially criminalized under the existing laws. This can be observed in the IPC, where acts in any form, spreading disharmony or feelings of enmity, are penalized under Section 153B. Current crises of mob violence are not due to the absence of any provisions, but lack of implementation in the best suited way. In the scenario where existing laws are exhaustively assessed in terms of mob violence and the experiment fails, new laws could make their way for deliberations. The new law against mob violence must be strengthened officially and facilitate victim empowerment (Bhat, 2018). A more victim-centric perspective must be implemented; currently, the problem of violence is a rise of hate violence against minorities, particularly Muslims, Dalits, and migrants from the Northeast.

Supreme Court had claimed that the state failed to address the mob lynching and recommended formulating adequate laws to tackle the problem. They also focused on the victims by providing victim compensation and witness protection guidelines. The authors found the case very useful, as it widened the horizon to cover mob lynching under the ambit of hate crimes and enabled this study to show the necessity as to why the people should consider mob violence as the class of hate crimes.

The empirical method to study the subject topic was always fruitful; the section of youth members were subjected to a questionnaire with typical questions involving as to what a hate crime was. This study had shown that hate crimes in groups were highly disruptive to peace in society. The study also showed the perceptions and sensitivity of young generations toward social evil like hate crimes (Craig & Waldo, 2018). After analyzing studies like these, the authors of this book formulated a more specific and complex questionnaire with a large sample focused on Northeast Indians residing in metropolitan cities.

Systematic analysis of problems faced by the Northeast Indians in metro cities was the main aim of this project, which included harassment, ill-treatment, racial attacks, etc. This meant that lack of human values could be observed as a cause of meting this kind of treatment to these sections of society due to their phenotypes and geographical position in society (Aamareswaram, 2017). However, authors of this book studied various solutions focusing on human values and tolerance and covered other aspects related to the involvement of society, government, and the role of police authorities in curbing racial hate crimes against Northeast Indians residing in metro cities.

1.3 Statement of the Problem

The present study was premised on the fact that there is a growing trend of the cases related to prejudice and violence against the people of Northeast regions, forming what we may call "hate crime." Cases like the murder of Nido Tania (from Arunachal Pradesh), Souloni Akha (from Manipur), the suspicious death of Richard Loitam (Manipur), and the murder and attempted rape of Ramchanphy Hongray (a girl from Nagaland), among others, represented the growing intolerance in various metro cities toward these people. The daily instances of hatred culminated in severe instances of violence, which needed a thorough probe to evolve objective information and data on this subject. The present book was, thus, an effort to map the experiences and vulnerabilities of people of Northeast regions in metro cities in their interaction with educational institutions and workplaces. The data for this study was collected on various aspects of prejudice, violence, and intolerance faced by Northeast people.

Examining legal provisions and the role of institutions in controlling and preventing such crimes was also done, and measures to control such violence were formulated at the end of this study.

1.4 Objectives

- To study the profiles of people from the Northeast part of the country residing in metropolitan cities like Delhi, Mumbai, Hyderabad, Pune, Chennai, and Bangalore
- To examine the various kinds of security concerns and experiences faced by Northeastern people in their daily lives while residing in metro cities
- To identify reasons behind the acts of prejudice and violence (hate crimes) against people from Northeastern
- To understand the nature of secondary victimization faced by the Northeastern people during post-victimization stages.
- To critically evaluate the existing legal framework to comprehensively deal with the cases of prejudices and violence faced by people from the Northeastern states
- To suggest preventive measures for minimizing the above-stated concerns that the law enforcement agencies could take

1.5 Hypotheses and Research Questions

Based on the in-depth literature review and objectives of the research study, the following hypotheses and research questions were formulated:

Hn01 = Geographical indifference, physical appearance, and the cultural difference had led to an increase in prejudicial attitudes against Northeast people residing in metro cities.

Hn02 = Dearth of legal protection toward Northeast people had led to an increase in hate crime incidences.

1.5.1 Research Questions

- Do the people from Northeast India face more prejudices and violence than people from mainland cities?
- Is there a dearth of appropriate legal provisions to tackle the causes of prejudices and violence against people from Northeastern states?

- Do people from Northeastern states face more prejudices and violence in metro cities, viz. Delhi, Mumbai, Chennai, Hyderabad, Pune, and Bengaluru, in comparison to the atrocities in small cities?
- Had the lack of legal provisions resulted in an insensitive attitude of the police toward people from the Northeast?

1.6 Operational/Conceptual Definitions

Hate crime: According to this study, hate crime means prejudice and violence faced by the people from Northeastern states living in the metro cities of India.

Northeast: The easternmost region of India consists of the following population – the Mongoloids, the Indo-Aryans, the Australians or Austrians and the Dravidians, and a minor group of some immigrant population.

1.6.1 Key Variables Employed

This research design was formulated to elaborate on the relationship between independent and dependent variables. For the present research study, independent and dependent variables were differentiated and analyzed to achieve the study's aims. The independent variables for the project were the *prejudices* that the public has toward Northeast Indians in metro cities and the *legal protection* for the Northeastern people in metro cities against incidents of hate crime. *Prejudices* against the northeastern people were evaluated with the dependent variable *prejudicial attitude* that Northeast people face. *Legal developments* were studied with the dependent variable *hate crime incidents* against Northeast Indian people in metro cities.

Prejudices of the public regarding the Northeastern population were determined by analyzing the prejudices based on geographical differences, cultural differences, and physical appearance. The *prejudicial attitude* of the police while handling hate crime incidents was analyzed with the independent variable to examine any connection between the two. *Legal protection* against hate crime incidents was established by evaluating the substantive and procedural legal safeguards reaching the Northeast people. This was studied regarding the *hate crime incidents* in the six metro cities against Northeast Indians.

This research design was formulated to explain and explore the nexus between the independent and dependent variables. Since the issue of atrocities and injustice against Northeast Indians in a metro city was a rapidly growing concern, it became imperative that every critical aspect revolving around such incidents was examined. Understanding the true picture of whether prejudices regarding geographical differences, cultural differences, or physical appearance affect the behavior they received from legal stakeholders, like the police helped us understand the root cause of the problem. Legal development was also another critical factor that was taken into account for this research. It became essential to interpret the connection between hate crime incidents and the legal provisions that are currently in place. This enabled the researchers to deduce whether there was a need for further legal amendments and statutory creation or whether the current scenario was appropriate for the issue.

1.7 Research Methodology

1.7.1 Research Design

Universe of the Study
The current study samples were from Northeast people and the general population residing in six metro cities.

The Locale of the Study
Metro cities with relatively higher cases of atrocities against people from the Northeast were selected as the universe for research work. The six states studied under this current study were Delhi, Mumbai, Chennai, Hyderabad, Pune, and Bengaluru.

1.7.2 Research Methods

As per the requirements of the objectives of the research and the hypotheses of the research, this book adhered to both empirical and doctrinal research methods of research methodology.

1.7.2.1 Empirical Research Methods

To study and analyze the prejudice and violence (hate crimes) faced by the people from Northeastern states living in the metro cities of India (Delhi, Mumbai, Chennai, Hyderabad, Pune, and Bengaluru), the researchers had carried out empirical research in all the abovementioned metro cities. To frame a research tool, a pilot study was conducted with 15 individuals from the Northeastern states. A structured interview schedule, as well as a questionnaire, was crafted after the proposed testing of the tool.

1.7.2.2 Doctrinal Research Methods

The case study method was opted by the research team to understand how the respondents considered, interpreted, and gathered the concept of hate crimes. This allowed the researchers to study various perceptions associated with the concept of hate crime and their influence on the behavior of Northeast people. It also helped the authors to understand how laws are interpreted. The primary outcome of the case study method was to give in-depth, real-world information on a complex issue. In addition, the study aimed to understand the prejudices associated with hate crimes against Northeast people. This was achieved by collecting and triangulating a wide range of data sources for testing the hypothesis.

1.7.3 Sample Size and Sampling Method

This book was proposed to analyze the prejudices and violence (hate crimes) faced by the people from Northeastern states residing in the six metro cities of India – Delhi, Mumbai, Chennai, Hyderabad, Pune, and Bengaluru. The whole study was approached with the nonprobability sampling technique. First, the selection of the Northeastern population was based on the *purposive sampling technique*, as the study is concerned with only Northeastern people. Then, the individual sample was identified using the *snowball sampling technique* to build rapport and connect easily to get accurate information. A total of 1,200 respondents participated in this study, i.e., 200 respondents from each metro city.

The chart below gives a more detailed division of samples collected during the study (see Fig. 1.1).

So as to maintain a representative sample, the number of respondents from each Northeastern state living in different metro cities was maintained evenly, i.e., among 150 samples from each metro city, approximately 18 samples were collected from the respondents of each Northeastern state.

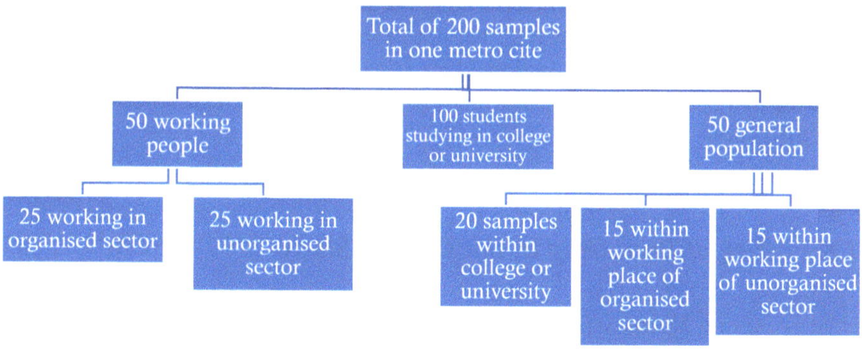

Fig. 1.1 Division of samples collected

1.7.4 *Tools and Techniques of Data Collection*

Since the study dealt with a sensitive issue, due care was taken by the research team during the data collection without hurting the respondents' sentiments. Therefore, respondent friendly tools and techniques were adopted to ease and share their experiences with different forms of violence and prejudice faced by them or someone closer to them. Therefore, the tools and techniques which were used in this study were as follows:

Interview Method
This study involved two sets of structured interview schedules:

(a) A structured interview schedule which was specially designed to record violence and prejudice faced by Northeastern people
(b) A structured interview schedule for the general population designed to record perceptions and opinions about Northeastern people

Both interview schedules were formulated based on the pilot study conducted in New Delhi on 50 samples. This helped the researchers check the schedule's reliability and validity.

Questionnaire Method
The structured interview schedules were then converted into Google forms, which were personally sent to the respondent's email id for data collection.

Data Collection
Data collection was done within 8 months, and a total of 1200 samples were collected from all six metropolitan cities.

1.8 Pretesting

An essential part of constructing the questionnaire process was its piloting, also known as pretesting. This involved testing our research instrument in conditions as similar as possible to the research, but not to report results but rather to check for glitches in the wording of questions, lack of clarity of instructions, etc. – in fact, anything that could impede the instrument's ability to collect data economically and systematically.

1.8.1 *Use of Pretesting in the Present Study*

Hate crimes on Northeasterners was not a vastly researched field in India which made it difficult for the researchers to accurately discern and check which questions would be fit for the study, i.e., those questions which could meet the aim of the research without hurting the sentiments of the Northeastern population in metro cities. The fear of hurting the sentiments of the people was inescapable since the issue revolved around the elements of their exploitation and social exclusion. Therefore, these matters had to be dealt with carefully, for which pretesting the questionnaire was deemed the best alternative. Moreover, this study was further conducted in a large base area, including major metro cities, considering a heavy sample size for research, which made it necessary to fool-proof the questionnaire that shaped the entire study on hate crimes on Northeastern Indians in metro cities.

1.8.2 Type of Pretesting

The pretesting conducted by the researchers was the "participating pretest," where the researchers told the respondents that the pretest was a practice run rather than simply asking the respondents to fill out the questionnaire. Participating in pretests usually involved an interview where respondents were asked to explain reactions to the question's form, wording, and order. This pretest helped the authors determine whether the questionnaire was understandable and effective in seeking genuine answers.

1.8.3 How the Pretest Was Conducted

A smaller number of participants or sample size was taken compared to the target sample size from all the metro cities. The authors covered this piloting process by taking samples from different areas within the research area. The participants included the Northeast Indian population and the general public – against whom two sets of questionnaires were presented. Although these questionnaires were similar in context, the independent variable that differentiated the two was whether or not the participant belonged to the Northeast region of India. This altered the questionnaire in the sense of the point of view or the perspective in which the participants viewed or witnessed hate crimes happening against the Northeast population of India in metro cities. Therefore, the authors conducting pretesting of the questionnaire approached the participants individually and asked the enumerated questions. As the participants answered the questions, the authors consequently analyzed whether the questionnaire was apt for fulfilling the study's objectives on hate crimes against Northeast Indians in metro cities.

1.8.4 *The Technique of Pretesting Used*

Expert Review This method was used in evaluating the questionnaires. It was an informal and individually based expert review. Each participating researcher independently conducted an expert review on an assigned questionnaire and determined whether they thought each questionnaire item was problematic. The questionnaire review form was designed so that each item was accompanied by a "problem indicator box," which the researcher marked if they perceived a potential problem with the item for either the interviewer or the respondent. Space was also provided under each question for the researcher to write specific notes about the suspected problem. No other specific instructions were provided to the researchers conducting the expert review, except for a short description of the overall questionnaire goals.

Result of Pretesting From pretesting, the researchers could check the flow and order in which the questionnaire was built and the extent to which it was efficient and clear to the participants. The questionnaire constructed was adequate in proceeding with a flow and ease that the participants could easily comprehend. Furthermore, the researchers did not face any haphazardness in following the order of the questionnaire. Also, skip patterns to questions written in the questionnaire were observed to be less, considering the questionnaire contained more than 25 questions. However, the questions that were susceptible to being skipped were mostly where the participants were asked to describe the hate crime incident that happened to them precisely. Nevertheless, the participants outlined the particulars of such incidents, which solved the purpose of the questionnaire.

The questionnaire/interview schedule was also tested for reliability and validity. A questionnaire was reliable when all the questions were understood and answered in the same way by all the respondents. Validity was determined by how well the questionnaire measured the concept(s) it was intended to measure. Through pretesting, the researchers concluded that the questions were answered in the same sense and in the same way by all the respondents. Hence, the questionnaire and interview schedule met the study's objectives by covering all the aspects of hate crimes against Northeast Indians in metro cities.

1.9 Data Analysis and Report Writing

The data collected in the current study was analyzed using inferential statistical methods. The data analysis involved transferring the coded data on the Statistical Package for Social Sciences (SPSS) Sheet, and then appropriate methods/tests were administered to test the hypothesis. The methods/tests applied were correlations coefficient (R), coefficient of determination, and Pearson's Chi-square. There were six key variables in the study, with the formulation of 72 frequency tables, 19 cross-tabulation tables, and seven tables concerning advanced tests (will be changed as per the data requirement).

1.10 Significance of the Study

India is a country that is well known for its unity in diversity. However, despite the prevalence of unity in diversity, recent news reports demonstrated the insecure conditions under which people, especially the youth, from the Northeast region of India have to live within metro cities. Few surveys had revealed that Northeast communities considered the metro cities the most unsafe place in terms of ethnic discrimination. The study helped analyze the prejudices and violence faced by people from Northeastern states and measures to counter them. The study also critically examined the existing legal framework and the effectiveness of measures taken by the government to counter such issues.

1.11 Limitations

1. Data collection was a little bit difficult due to the reluctance of the respondents to share information with the field investigators.
2. In some instances, the respondents made the investigators either wait for long hours or were made to make repeated visits before they were ready to share their experiences.
3. Prior research conducted in this area was relatively less, especially in the Indian context. Not many scholarly papers addressing the research problem were found.
4. Analyzing the data collected by the research team was quite challenging and time-consuming.

1.12 Picturesque of the Study

For the convenience of the readers, the current study was divided into seven chapters. This chapter covered the introduction with the research methodology applied by the research team. Chapter 2 focused on profile analysis of the Northeast people residing in metro cities where the variables used were gender, age, region, and tribe. Chapter 3 discussed the rationale behind security concerns regarding hate crimes committed against Northeast people. Chapter 4 focused on secondary victimization during post-victimization stages. Chapter 5 analyzed the legal development and services against hate crimes toward Northeast people. Chapter 6 covered the findings and suggestions proposed by the research team. Chapter 7 provided a summary and conclusion, followed by the bibliography and annexure.

References

Aamareshwaran, D. N. (2017). Problems of North-east people in metro cities of India: Need of human values for happy and healthy life. *International Journal of Education and Multidisciplinary Studies*, 103–108.

Barkataki, T. (2017). *Discrimination and the rising of Northeast – A long way to go* (pp. 1–7).

Baruah, S. (2008, September). India and its Northeast: A new politics of race. *South Asia Citizens Web*. Retrieved June 1, 2020, from http://www.sacw.net/article63.html

Bezbaruah, M. (2014). *Racial discrimination against North-East Indians*.

Bhat, M. A. (2018, August 14). *Hindustan Times*. Retrieved October, 2019, from https://www.hindustantimes.com/analysis/mob-lynching-should-be-categorised-as-a-class-of-hate-crimes/story-0NvzhshQfKg6h2dhm3NXRM.html

Bijukumar, V. (2013, July). Social exclusion & ethnicity in Northeast India. *The Nehu Journal, 9*, 19–35.

Chakraborti, N., & Garland, J. (2012). Reconceptualizing hate crime victimization through the lens of vulnerability and difference. *Theoretical Criminology, 16*(4), 499–514. https://doi.org/10.1177/1362480612439432

Chauhan, J. B. (2017). *Hate speech*. Law Commission of India.

Craig, K. M., & Waldo, C. R. (2018). So what's hate crime anyway? Young adult's perception of hate crimes, victims & perpetrators. *Law & Human Behavior, 20*(2), 113–129.

Gerstenfeld, P. B. (2011). *Hate crimes: Causes, controls & controversies* (2nd ed.). Sage.

Hazarika, S. (2017, August 11). *Hindustan Times*. Retrieved February 2019, from https://www.hindustantimes.com/analysis/discrimination-being-north-eastern-and-indian-ness/story-s8Y33kar75WFkH4CdGkV8H.html

Hindpal Singh Bhui, D. S. (2009). *Race and criminal justice*. Sage.

Hurd, H. M. (2001). Why liberals should hate – Hate crime legislation. *Law and Philosophy, 20*(2). https://doi.org/10.2307/3505240

Jain, N. (2016). Northeast India's multi ethnicities: Dominant issues and problems. *International Journal of Humanities & Social Science Studies*, 275–285.

Karukus, P., & Goregenli, M. (2011). Who is guilty? Undergraduate students' attitude towards, hate crime based on sexual orientation. *International Journal of Arts and Science*, 253–264.

Leonard, C. R. (2014). *Beyond hate: White power & popular culture*. Dorset Press.

Lyons, C. J. (2006, March). Stigma, or sympathy? Attributions of fault to hate crimes and offenders. *Social Psychology Quarterly, 69*, 39–59.

McDuie-Ra, D. (2012). *North-east migrants in Delhi: Race, refugee & retail*. International Institute for Asian Studies.

McDuie-Ra, D. (2013). Leaving the North-east borderland: placemaking & the inward pull of citizenship in India. *Eurasia Border Review*, 1–17.

McDuie-Ra, D. (2016, January 14). 'Is India racist?' Murder, migration and Mary Kom. *South Asia: Journal of South Asian Studies*, 304–319.

Murakami, T. K. (2004). Hate crimes. *Journal of Gender and the Law, 5*, 63–75.

National Institute of Justice. (n.d.). *Hate crime*. Retrieved August, 2020, from https://www.nij.gov/topics/crime/hate-crime/pages/welcome.aspx

OSCE. (2014). *Prosecuting hate crimes* (pp. 1–101). Office for Democratic Institution & Human Rights.

OSCE – ODIHR. (2018, November 16). *What is hate crime*. Retrieved January 30, 2019, from http://hatecrime.osce.org/what-hate-crime

OSCE – ODIHR. (2019). *What is hate crime*. Retrieved January 30, 2019, from http://hatecrime.osce.org/what-hate-crime

Raj, S. (2016, December 1). From marginalisation to sterotypes- 'North-East Indian media: Evidences from focus group discussions in Manipur'. Journal of North-East Indian Studies, *6*(2), 70–79.

Ramesh, B. P. (2012, June 2). strangers in their own land: Migrants from the North-east in Delhi. Economic and Political Weekly, *47*, 35–40.
Reuter, N. (2009). *Hate crimes, a practical guide*. OSCE/ODIHR.
Samson, K. (2017). North-East & Chinky: Continuance of racism in India. *Journal of Developmental Practice*, 20–28.
Samuel, J. (1993). Language & nationality in North-East. *Economic & Political Weekly, 28*, 91–92.
Thakur, D. (2009). *Tribal law and administration*. Deep & Deep Publications Pvt. Ltd.
Thounaojam, S. (2012). A preface to racial discourse in India: North-East and mainland. *Economic & Political Weekly*. Retrieved August 12, 2019, from https://www.jstor.org/stable/23251789
Wolfe, Z. J. (2014). *Hate crimes law to*. Thompson Reuters.

Chapter 2
Analysis of Profile of Northeast Population of India Living in Metropolitan Cities

2.1 Introduction

This chapter offers a preliminary analysis of the data collected from six cities, i.e., Pune, Mumbai, Hyderabad, Chennai, Bangalore, and Delhi. The findings were discussed by analyzing the Northeast population profiles in terms of gender, age group, tribes, region, and occupation. The findings of this chapter draw out the relationship between two categorical variables. To describe the relationship between these variables, the researchers conducted cross-tabulation. The cross-table formulated describes the number of rows and columns in the tables provided below:

where
R = number of the categories for the row variable
C = number of the categories for the column variable

Kindly note that the data of all six metro cities were individually analyzed in this chapter for better insight into the profile of the Northeast population.

Table 2.1 consists of a cross-tabulation for Bangalore City. Figure 2.1 gives a graphical representation of the male to female and gender ratio in Bangalore. Through this, we could quickly observe the interaction between the two variables mentioned above. Here, the row variable was age group (in years), and the column variable was gender.

The proportion of males between the age group (in years) of 18 and 22 years was 25.9% or 21/67 and of females was 66.7% or 46/67. The proportion of males between the age group (in years) of 23 and 30 years was 66.7% or 54/70 and of females was 23.2% or 16/70. The proportion of males between the age group (in years) of 31 and 40 years was 6.2% or 5/12 and of females was 10.1% or 7/12. The proportion of males in the age group (in years) of 41 and above years was 1.2% or 1/1 and of females was 0% or 0/1.

G. S. Bajpai et al., *Hate Crime in India*,
https://doi.org/10.1007/978-3-031-30522-1_2

Table 2.1 Distribution of Northeast people between the age group (in years)* gender residing in Bangalore

			Gender		Total
			Male	Female	
Age group	18–22	N	21	46	67
		% of total	14.0	30.7	44.7
	23–30	N	54	16	70
		% of total	36.0	10.7	46.7
	31–40	N	5	7	12
		% of total	3.3	4.7	8.0
	41 and above	N	1	0	1
		% of total	0.7	0.0	0.7
Total		N	81	69	150
		% of total	54.0	46.0	100.0

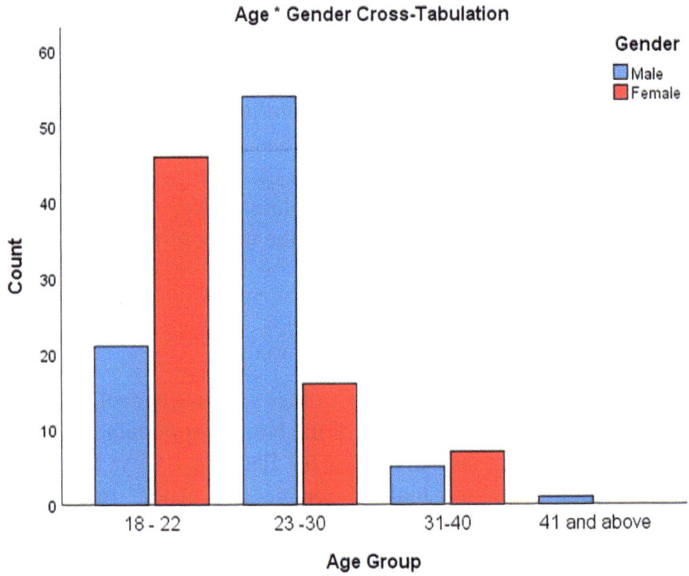

Fig. 2.1 Age group (in years) to gender

The total males (81) and females (69) were considered samples for the study in Bangalore. This shows that the Northeast population residing in Bangalore was more between the age group (in years) of 23 and 30 years. Out of which, males were more between the age group (in years) of 23 and 30 years and females between 18 and 22 years.

In Bangalore, data from the people of the following tribes was collected and studied: Naga (2), Tangkhul (4), Meitei (2), ST (1), Lotha (3), Nyishi (6), Mao (2), Garo (10), Khasi (6), Jaintia (1), Bodo (5), Adi (7), Aao (7), Deori (3), Bhutiya (3), Assamese (1), Halam (2), Kuki (5), Chakhesang (2), and Angami (4) tribes were

Table 2.2 Distribution of Northeast people between the age group (in years) * gender residing in Chennai city

			Gender		
			Male	Female	Total
Age group_Chennai	18–22	N	8	17	25
		% of total	5.3	11.3	16.7
	23–30	N	68	47	115
		% of total	45.3	31.3	76.7
	31–40	N	7	3	10
		% of total	4.7	2.0	6.7
Total		N	83	67	150
		% of total	55.3	44.7	100.0

found less in number. Mostly the Northeast population belonged to the Manipur region (33) of the Tangkhul Naga tribe (12) in Bangalore City. The total sample size was 150.

Table 2.2 consists of a cross-tab for Chennai City. Figure 2.2 gives a graphical representation of the male to female and gender ratio in the city of Chennai. Through it, we could quickly observe the interaction between the two variables mentioned above. Here, the row variable was age group (in years), and the column variable was gender.

The proportion of males between the age group (in years) of 18 and 22 years was 9.6% or 8/25 and of females was 25.4% or 17/25. The proportion of males in the age group (in years) of 23–30 years was 81.9%, or 68/115, and females were 70.1% or 47/115. The proportion of males between the age group (in years) of 31 and 40 years was 8.4% or 7/10 and of females was 4.5% or 3/10.

The proportion of males between the age group (in years) of 41 and above years was 0 and of females was 0; hence, the values were hidden. The total males (83) and females (67) were considered samples for the study in Bangalore. This shows that the Northeast population residing in Chennai was more between the age group (in years) of 23 and 30 years for both males and females.

In Chennai, data from the people of the following tribes was collected and studied: Naga (2), Meitei (1), ST (7), Lotha (2), Nyishi (0), Mao (1), Garo (8), Khasi (3), Jaintia (0), Bodo (0), Adi (0), Aao (2), Deori (0), Bhutiya (0), Assamese (0), Halam (0), Kuki (0), Chakhesang (6), and Angami (4) tribes were found less in number. Mostly the Northeast population belonged to the Manipur region (37) of the Tangkhul Naga tribe (12) in Chennai City. The total sample size was 150.

Table 2.3 consists of a cross-tab for New Delhi. Figure 2.3 gives a graphical representation of the male to female and gender ratio in New Delhi. Through it, we could quickly observe the interaction between the two variables mentioned above. Here, the row variable was age group (in years), and the column variable was gender.

The proportion of males between the age group (in years) of 18 and 22 years was 39.7% or 29/76 and of females was 61.0% or 47/76. The proportion of males between the age group (in years) of 23 and 30 years was 50.7% or 37/59 and of

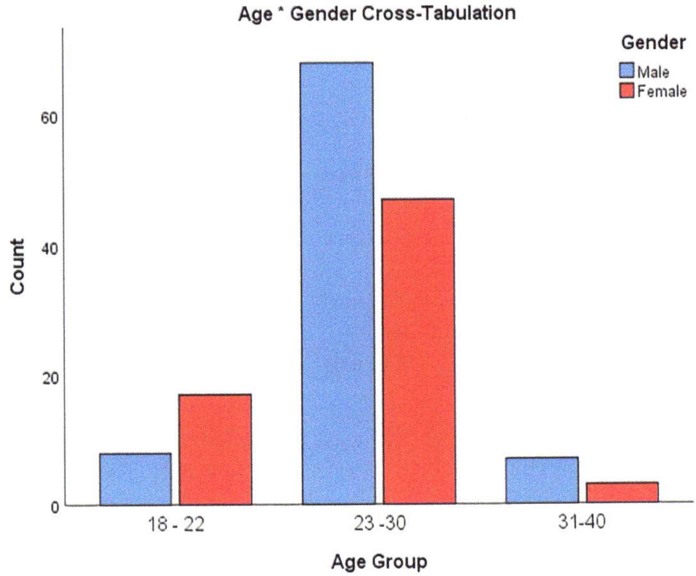

Fig. 2.2 Age group (in years) to gender

Table 2.3 Distribution of Northeast people between the age group (in years) * gender residing in New Delhi

			Gender		
			Male	Female	Total
Age group	18–22	N	29	47	76
		% of total	19.3	31.3	50.7
	23–30	N	37	22	59
		% of total	24.7	14.7	39.3
	3–40	N	7	6	13
		% of total	4.7	4.0	8.7
	41 and above	N	0	2	2
		% of total	0.0	1.3	1.3
Total		N	73	77	150
		% of total	48.7	51.3	100.0

females was 28.6% or 22/59. The proportion of males between the age group (in years) of 31 and 40 years was 9.6% or 7/13 and of females was 7.8% or 6/13.

The proportion of males between the age group (in years) of 41 and above years was 0% or 0/2 and of females was 2.6% or 2/2. The total males (73) and females (77) were considered as samples for the study in New Delhi. This shows that the Northeast population residing in New Delhi was more between the age group (in years) of 23 and 30 years. Out of which, males were more between the age group (in years) of 23 and 30 years and females between 18 and 22 years.

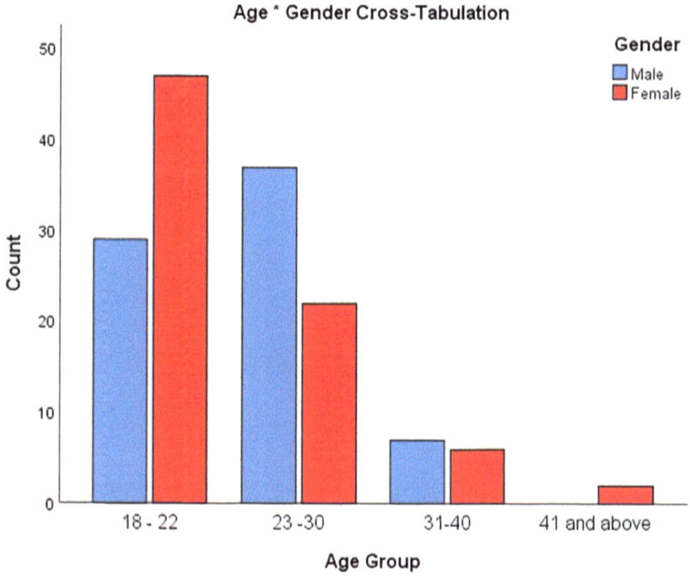

Fig. 2.3 Age group (in years) to gender

Table 2.4 Distribution of Northeast people between the age group (in years) * gender residing in Hyderabad City

			Gender		
			Male	Female	Total
Age group	18–22	N	18	28	46
		% of total	12.0	18.7	30.7
	23–30	N	37	36	73
		% of total	24.7	24.0	48.7
	31–40	N	14	12	26
		% of total	9.3	8.0	17.3
	41 and above	N	2	3	5
		% of total	1.3	2.0	3.3
Total		N	71	79	150
		% of total	47.3	52.7	100.0

In New Delhi, data from the people of the following tribes was collected and studied: Naga (5), Meitei (6), ST (13), Lotha (1), Nyishi (5), Mao (4), Garo (7), Khasi (3), Jaintia (1), Bodo (1), Adi (0), Aao (0), Deori (0), Bhutiya (5), Assamese (6), Halam (2), Chakhesang (0), and Angami (0) tribes were found less or negligible in number. Mostly the Northeast population belonged to the Manipur region (40) of the Kuki tribe (15) in New Delhi. The total sample size was 150.

Table 2.4 consists of a cross-tab for Hyderabad. Figure 2.4 gives a graphical representation of the male to female and gender ratio in the city of Hyderabad.

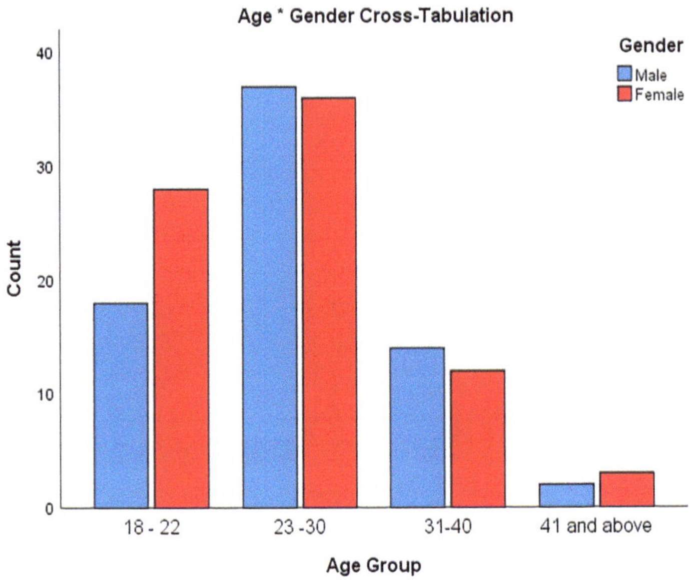

Fig. 2.4 Age group (in years) to gender

Through it, we could quickly observe the interaction between the two variables mentioned above. Here, the row variable was age group (in years), and the column variable was gender.

The proportion of males in the age group (in years) of 18–22 years was 25.4%, or 18/46, and females were 35.4% or 28/46. The proportion of males between the age group (in years) of 23 and 30 years was 52.1% or 37/73 and of females was 45.6% or 36/73. The proportion of males in the age group (in years) of 31–40 years was 19.7%, or 14/26, and females were 15.2% or 12/26. The proportion of males in the age group (in years) of 41 and above years was 2.8% or 2/5 and of females was 3.8% or 3/5.

The total males (71) and females (79) were considered samples for the study in Hyderabad. This shows that the Northeast population residing in Hyderabad was more between the age group (in years) of 23 and 30 years. Out of which, males and females were more between the age group (in years) of 23 and 30 years.

In Hyderabad, data from the people of the following tribes was collected and studied: Naga (0), Meitei (0), ST (3), Lotha (2), Nyishi (0), Mao (1), Garo (2), Khasi (0), Jaintia (0), Bodo (0), Adi (0), Aao (11), Deori (0), Bhutiya (0), Assamese (0), Halam (0), Chakhesang (8), Angami (2), and Sumi (1) tribes were found less or negligible in number. Mostly the Northeast population belonged to the Mizoram region of the Mazo tribe (14) in Hyderabad. The total sample size was 150.

Table 2.5 consists of a cross-tab for Mumbai. Figure 2.5 gives a graphical representation of the male to female and gender ratio in the city of Mumbai. Through it, we could quickly observe the interaction between the two variables mentioned

Table 2.5 Distribution of Northeast people between the age group (in years) * gender residing in Mumbai

			Gender			
			0	Male	Female	Total
Age group	0	N	1	1	0	2
		% of total	0.7	0.7	0.0	1.3
	18–22	N	0	12	19	31
		% of total	0.0	8.0	12.7	20.7
	23–30	N	0	41	53	94
		% of total	0.0	27.3	35.3	62.7
	31–40	N	0	10	8	18
		% of total	0.0	6.7	5.3	12.0
	41 and above	N	0	2	3	5
		% of total	0.0	1.3	2.0	3.3
Total		N	1	66	83	150
		% of total	0.7	44.0	55.3	100.0

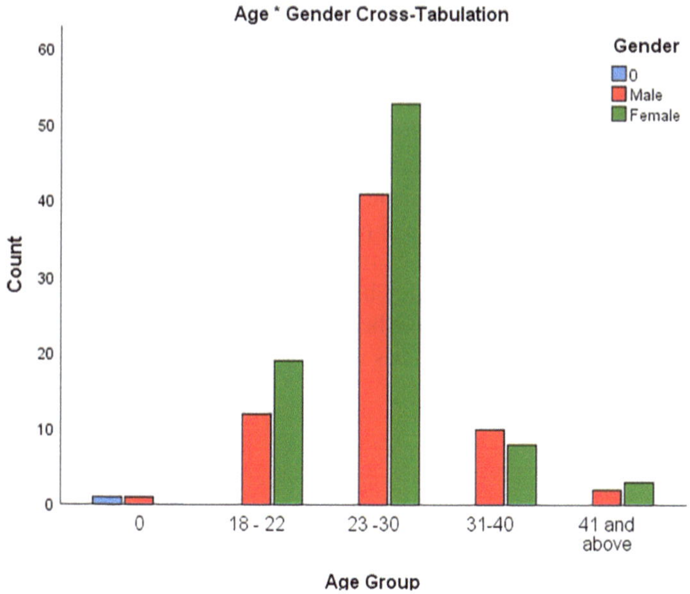

Fig. 2.5 Age group (in years) to gender

above. Here, the row variable was age group (in years), and the column variable was gender.

The proportion of males between the age group (in years) of 18 and 22 years was 18.2% or 12/31 and of females was 22.9% or 19/31. The proportion of males between the age group (in years) of 23 and 30 years was 62.1% or 41/94 and of females was 63.9% or 53/94. The proportion of males between the age group (in years) of 31 and 40 years was 15.2%, or 10/18, and of females was 9.6% or 8/18. The proportion of males between the age group (in years) of 41 and above was 3% and of females was 1%.

The total males (66) and females (83) were considered samples for the study in Hyderabad. This shows that the Northeast population residing in Mumbai was more between the age group (in years) of 23 and 30 years. Out of which, males and females were more between the age group (in years) of 23 and 30 years.

In Mumbai, data from the people of the following tribes was collected and studied: Naga (6), Tangkhul Nagar (20), Meitei (10), ST (3), Lotha (1), Nyishi (2), Mao (1), Garo (0), Khasi (0), Jaintia (0), Bodo (1), Adi (0), Aao (1), Deori (0), Bhutiya (0), Assamese (1), Halam (0), Chakhesang (0), Angami (0), Sumi (0), Chakma (1), and Apatani (2); tribes were found less or negligible in number. Mostly, the Northeast population belonged to the Manipur region (118) of the Tangkhul tribe (73) in Mumbai. The total sample size was 150.

Table 2.6 consists of cross-tabulation for Pune City. Figure 2.6 gives a graphical representation of the male to female and gender ratio in the city of Pune. Through it, we could quickly observe the interaction between the two variables mentioned above. Here, the row variable was age group (in years), and the column variable was gender.

The proportion of males between the age group (in years) of 18 and 22 years was 41.7% or 30/63 and of females was 33% or 33/63. The proportion of males between the age group (in years) of 23 and 30 years was 51.4% or 37/78 and of females was 52.6% or 41/78. The proportion of males between the age group (in years) of 31 and 40 years was 4.2% or 3/6 and of females was 3.8% or 3/6.

The proportion of males in the age group (in years) of 41 and above years was 2.8%, or 2/3, and of females was 1.3% or 1/3. The total males (72) and females (78) were considered samples for the study in Hyderabad. This shows that the Northeast population residing in Pune was more between the age group (in years) of 23 and 30 years. Out of which, males and females were more between the age group (in years) of 23 and 30 years.

Table 2.6 Distribution of Northeast people – age group* gender residing in Pune

			Gender		
			Male	Female	Total
Age group (in years)	18–22	N	30	33	63
		% of total	20.0	22.0	42.0
	23–30	N	37	41	78
		% of total	24.7	27.3	52.0
	31–40	N	3	3	6
		% of total	2.0	2.0	4.0
	41 and above	N	2	1	3
		% of total	1.3	0.7	2.0
Total		N	72	78	150
		% of total	48.0	52.0	100.0

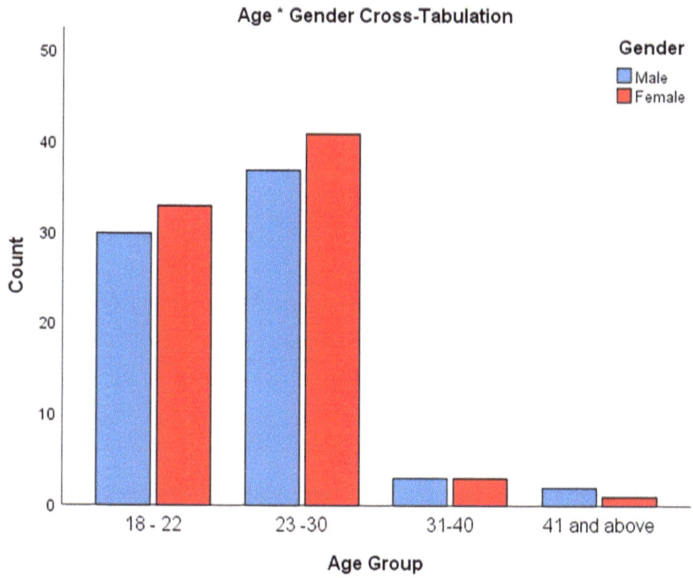

Fig. 2.6 Age group (in years) to gender

In Pune, data from the people of the following tribes was collected and studied: Naga (4), Meitei (2), ST (3), Lotha (1), Nyishi (0), Mao (3), Garo (7), Khasi (3), Jaintia (0), Bodo (0), Adi (1), Aao (2), Deori (0), Bhutiya (1), Assamese (7), Halam (1), Chakhesang (3), Angami (8), and Sumi (4). Mostly, the Northeast population belonged to the Manipur (66) region of Tangkhul Naga and Mizo tribe (10) in Pune. The total sample size was 150.

Figure 2.7 shows the various occupations held by the Northeast population residing across six metropolitan cities. In continuation to Fig. 2.7, Fig. 2.8 was a graphical representation of the various occupations by the Northeast people residing in six metro cities. Again, the row variable was occupation (4 categories: student, self-employed, private, and public), and the column variable was city residing (New Delhi, Chennai, Bangalore, Hyderabad, Pune, and Mumbai. The total sample taken per city was 150 and of all six cities was 900.

The above table shows that 62.3% were students, 19.9% were working in the private sector, 12.4% were self-employed, 5.2% were in Public, and 0.1% did not answer the question. Out of this, city-wise, Pune City reported the highest student percentage (84.7%), followed by Hyderabad (73.3%), Chennai (66%), New Delhi (59.3%), and Mumbai (45.3%). With reference to other occupations city-wise, the Northeast population was more involved in the private sector (41.3%, Bangalore), self-employed (28%, Mumbai), followed by public (12.7%, Chennai).

Occupation * Metro City Crosstabulation

			Which metro city are you residing in?						
			Pune	Mumbai	New Delhi	Bangalore	Chennai	Hyderabad	Total
Occupation	0	Count	0	1	0	0	0	0	1
		% within Which metro city are you residing in?	0.0%	0.7%	0.0%	0.0%	0.0%	0.0%	0.1%
	Student	Count	127	68	89	68	99	110	561
		% within Which metro city are you residing in?	84.7%	45.3%	59.3%	45.3%	66.0%	73.3%	62.3%
	Self-employed	Count	6	42	17	17	19	11	112
		% within Which metro city are you residing in?	4.0%	28.0%	11.3%	11.3%	12.7%	7.3%	12.4%
	Private	Count	14	31	38	62	13	21	179
		% within Which metro city are you residing in?	9.3%	20.7%	25.3%	41.3%	8.7%	14.0%	19.9%
	Public	Count	3	8	6	3	19	8	47
		% within Which metro city are you residing in?	2.0%	5.3%	4.0%	2.0%	12.7%	5.3%	5.2%
Total		Count	150	150	150	150	150	150	900
		% within Which metro city are you residing in?	100.0%	100.0%	100.0%	100.0%	100.0%	100.0%	100.0%

Fig. 2.7 Various occupations of Northeast people across all six metro cities

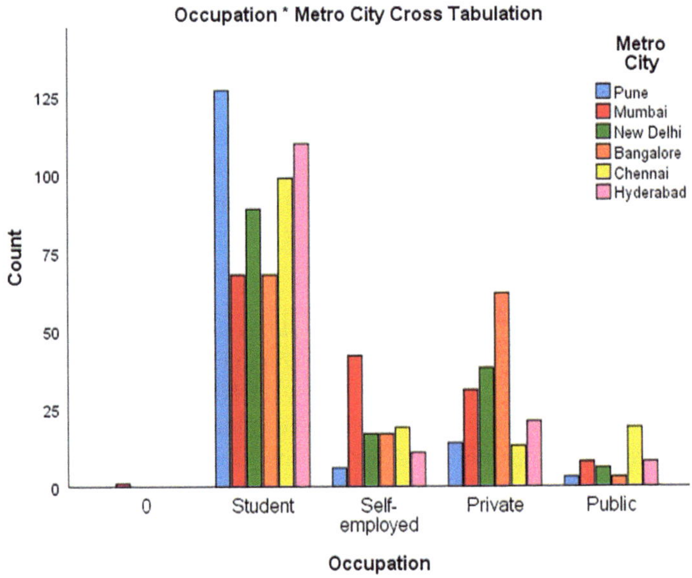

Fig. 2.8 Occupation in metro city

2.1.1 *Interpretation*

Thus, the inference drawn from this chapter was that primarily the Northeast population residing across all the six metro cities were students, followed by people working in the private sector. Generally, the population belonged to the age group of 23–30 years; of which, males were more in number compared to females. Mostly, the Northeast people residing in the six metro cities belong to Manipur and Mizoram regions and were of the Tangkhul Naga and Mizo tribes, respectively.

Chapter 3
Rationale Behind Security Concerns to Hate Crimes

3.1 Introduction

The reasons identified and studied with respect to security concerns of hate crimes across six metropolitan cities had been further subjected to advanced statistical analysis so that the interaction of various variables could be ascertained. The data of both the target groups had been taken into account, i.e., of Northeast population and general population residing in the six metro cities. The researchers had tried to understand the security concerns of Northeast populations toward hate crimes.

This section further deals with the testing of the hypothesis ($_{Hn01)}$ mentioned in Chapter I and also helped to develop an understanding as to whether the increase in prejudicial attitude against Northeast people was dependent or independent on the reasons identified through this current study.

Hypothesis was reproduced below:

The second half of the chapter covers various forms of hate crime incidences witnessed by the Northeast population and general population residing in metro cities, awareness toward the concept of hate crimes, the problems associated with it, and the mental state of Northeast people during the commission of the incident. The reasons identified behind the security concerns of the Northeast population has been illustrated below.

3.1.1 Prejudice of Geographical Difference

In case of prejudice, i.e., *geographical difference*, the following responses were recorded.

Table 3.1 represents the total number of Northeast populations expressing whether they believe prejudices like geographical difference act as a security

G. S. Bajpai et al., *Hate Crime in India*,
https://doi.org/10.1007/978-3-031-30522-1_3

Table 3.1 Responses of Northeastern people related to security concerns residing in all six metropolitan cities

Prejudice in metro city		N	Percentage
Geographical difference the reason in Bangalore	0	40	26.7
	Geographical difference	30	20.0
	No geographical difference	80	53.3
Geographical difference the reason in Chennai	0	29	19.3
	Geographical difference	47	31.3
	No geographical difference	74	49.3
Geographical difference the reason in Delhi	0	38	25.3
	Geographical difference	31	20.7
	No geographical difference	81	54.0
Geographical difference the reason in Hyderabad	0	52	34.7
	Geographical difference	33	22.0
	No geographical difference	65	43.3
Geographical difference the reason in Mumbai	0	28	18.7
	Geographical difference	49	32.7
	No geographical difference	73	48.7
Geographical difference the reason in Pune	0	48	32.0
	Geographical difference	31	20.7
	No geographical difference	71	47.3
	Total	900	100.0

concern across all six metro cities. Within the population of Northeast people residing across all six cities, there was a set of individuals who did not respond to this, which was denoted by the numerical 0. For instance, in Bengaluru (26.7%), Chennai (19.3%), Delhi (25.3%), Hyderabad (34.7%), Mumbai (18.7%), and Pune (20.7%).

However, there were individuals within the Northeast population who believed that there was geographical difference leading to security threat against the Northeast people residing in the six metro cities. Around 31.3% in Chennai, 20% in Bengaluru, 20.7% in Delhi, 22% in Hyderabad, 32.7% in Mumbai, and 20.7% in Pune supported the same.

Another set of individuals believed that there wasn't any geographical difference which would cause them any security threat. This could be seen via responses across the six metro cities: Chennai (49.3%), Bengaluru (53.3%), Delhi (54.0%), Hyderabad (43.3%), Mumbai (48.7%), and Pune (47.3%).

Figure 3.1 represents a graphical view of the total percentage of the responses by Northeast people residing in six metro cities. The responses show that the Northeast population across six cities largely did not believe that geographical difference was a security threat to them.

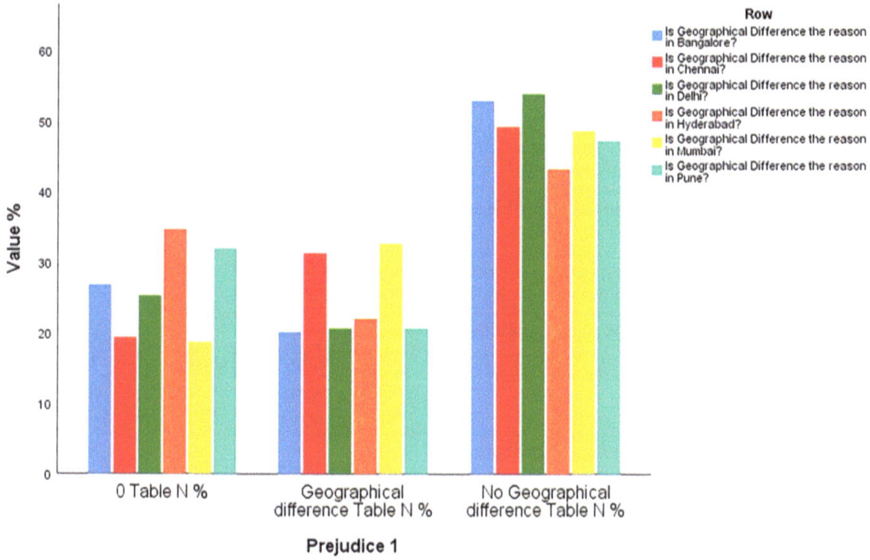

Fig. 3.1 Prejudice 1

3.1.1.1 Interpretation

From the above data, one could understand that most the Northeast people in metro cities do not believe that geographical differences were a ground for prejudice, and Delhi specifically had the most respondents agreeing for the same. Although, there was less percentage of Northeast people believing geographical difference was the reason for prejudicial behavior against them, Mumbai had a higher number of respondents than in other metro cities considering the reason for prejudices as geographical difference. Hence, it was pertinent to note that among the three reasons that could be plausible for prejudice against the Northeast Indians in metro cities, although the percentage being less, geographical difference remained the reason for prejudice, exclusion, and humiliation.

Table 3.2 represents the total number of general populations expressing whether they believed if prejudices like geographical difference acted as a security concern across all six metro cities.

Within the population of general public residing across all six cities, there was a set of individuals who did not to comment on this: Bengaluru (14.0%), Chennai (6.0%), Delhi (2.0%), Hyderabad (8.0%), Mumbai (6.0%), and Pune (18%).

However, there were individuals within the Northeast population who believed that there was geographical difference leading to security threat against the Northeast people residing in the six metro cities. Around (26.0%) in Chennai, Bengaluru (26.0%), Delhi (16.0%), Hyderabad (32.0%), Mumbai (42.0%), and Pune (36.0%) supported the same.

Table 3.2 Distribution according to general public residing in all six metropolitan cities

Prejudice		N	Percentage
Geographical difference, the major problem in Bangalore	0	7	14.0
	Geographical difference	13	26.0
	No geographical difference	30	60.0
Geographical difference, the major problem in Chennai	0	3	6.0
	Geographical difference	13	26.0
	No geographical difference	34	68.0
Geographical difference, the major problem in Delhi	0	1	2.0
	Geographical difference	8	16.0
	No geographical difference	41	82.0
Geographical difference, the major problem in Hyderabad	0	4	8.0
	Geographical difference	16	32.0
	No geographical difference	30	60.0
Geographical difference, the major problem in Mumbai	0	3	6.0
	Geographical difference	21	42.0
	No geographical difference	26	52.0
Geographical difference, the major problem in Pune	0	9	18.0
	Geographical difference	18	36.0
	No geographical difference	23	46.0
	Total	300	100.0

Another set of individuals believed that there wasn't any geographical difference which would cause them any security threat. This could be seen via responses across the six metro cities: Chennai (68.0%), Bengaluru (60.0%), Delhi (82.0%), Hyderabad (60.0%), Mumbai (52.0%), and Pune (46.0%).

Figure 3.2 represents a graphical view of the total percentage of the responses by general population residing in six metro cities. The responses show that the general population across the six cities largely did not believe that geographical difference was a security threat to them.

3.1.1.2 Interpretation

According to the above data, most percentage of general population believed that geographical difference was not the reason that the Northeast population in metro cities faced prejudice or differential treatment. Delhi was the city where most general people held this view. Apart from the majority of the respondents considering geographical difference as not being the reason for prejudice, there was certain

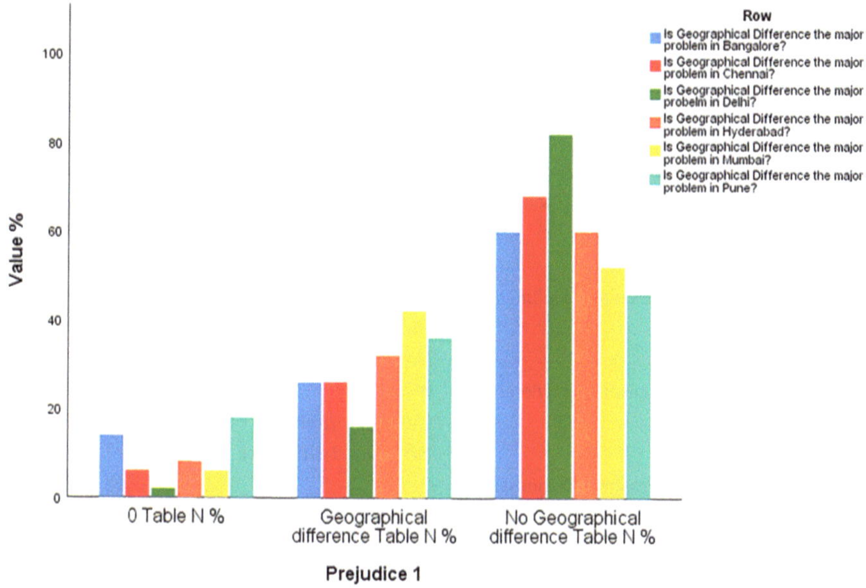

Fig. 3.2 Prejudice 1

percentage of people who believed that geographical difference was the cause for such a treatment against the Northeast people. Mumbai was the city where most respondents consider that geographical difference might be the reason of prejudices in metro cities.

3.1.2 *Prejudice of Cultural Difference*

In case of second prejudice, i.e., *cultural difference*, the following responses were recorded.

Table 3.3 represents the total number of Northeast population expressing whether they believe if prejudices like cultural difference acted as a security concern across all the six metro cities.

Within the population of Northeast people residing across all six cities, there was a set of individuals who did not comment: Bengaluru (26.7%), Chennai (19.3%), Delhi (25.3%), Hyderabad (34.7%), Mumbai (18.7%), and Pune (32.0%).

However, there were individuals within the Northeast population who believed that there was cultural difference leading to security threat against the Northeast people residing in six metro cities. Around (60.0%) in Chennai, Bengaluru (36.7%), Delhi (49.3%), Hyderabad (42.7%), Mumbai (62.7%), and Pune (43.3%) supported the same.

Table 3.3 Responses of Northeastern people related to security concerns residing in all six metropolitan cities

Prejudice		N	Percentage
Cultural difference the reason in Bangalore	0	40	26.7
	Cultural difference	55	36.7
	No cultural difference	55	36.7
Cultural difference the reason in Chennai	0	29	19.3
	Cultural difference	90	60.0
	No cultural difference	31	20.7
Cultural difference the reason in Delhi	0	38	25.3
	Cultural difference	74	49.3
	No cultural difference	38	25.3
Cultural difference the reason in Hyderabad	0	52	34.7
	Cultural difference	64	42.7
	No cultural difference	34	22.7
Cultural difference the reason in Mumbai	0	28	18.7
	Cultural difference	94	62.7
	No cultural difference	28	18.7
Cultural difference the reason in Pune	0	48	32.0
	Cultural difference	65	43.3
	No cultural difference	37	24.7
	Total	900	100.0

Another set of individuals believed that there wasn't any cultural difference which would cause them any security threat. That could be seen via responses across six metro cities like in Chennai (20.7%), Bengaluru (36.7%), Delhi (25.3%), Hyderabad (22.7%), Mumbai (18.7%), and Pune (24.7%).

Figure 3.3 represents graphical view of the total percentage of the responses by the Northeast people residing in the six metro cities. The responses show that the Northeast population across the six cities largely did believe that cultural difference was one of the security threats to them.

3.1.2.1 Interpretation

A higher percentage of the Northeast Indian people from metro cities believe that cultural difference was the reason for prejudice against them. More Northeast people in Mumbai had the view that cultural difference remains one of the reasons which had led to hate crime incidents in the city, whereas most northeast people in Bangalore believe that cultural differences between the people were not the primary reasons behind such crimes. That marked an identification to the fact that there was diversity in the Northeast population that was spread across the Indian subcontinent. The viewpoints of people differ in different cities and thus was visible in the data collected.

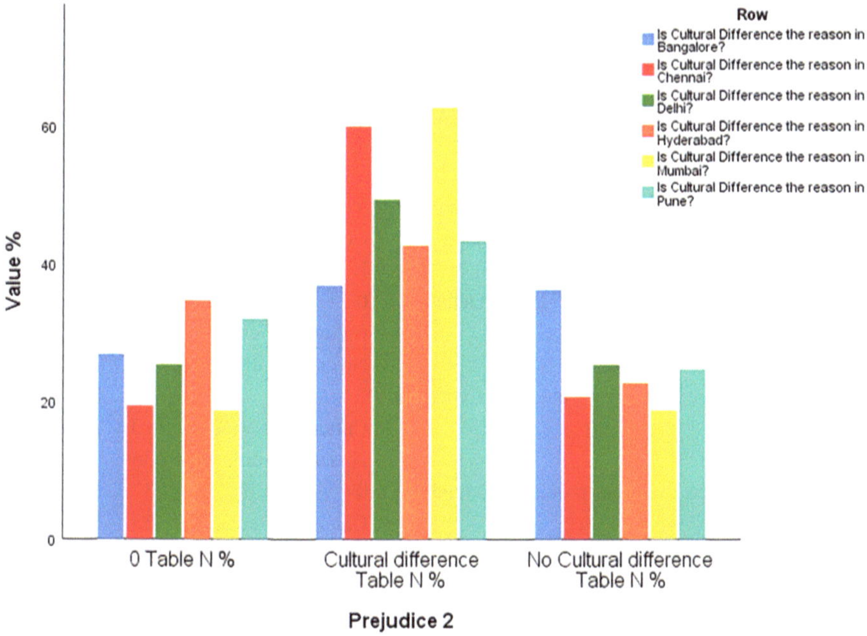

Fig. 3.3 Prejudice 2

Table 3.4 represents the total number of general populations expressing whether they believe that prejudices like cultural differences act as a security concern across all the six metro cities. Within the population of general public residing across all six cities, there was a set of individuals who did not comment on the same: Bengaluru (14.0%), Chennai (6.0%), Delhi (2.0%), Hyderabad (8.0%), Mumbai (6.0%), and Pune (18.0%).

However, there were individuals within the Northeast population who believed that cultural differences lead to security threats against the Northeast people residing in the six metro cities. Around (48.0%) in Chennai, Bengaluru (52.0%), Delhi (58.0%), Hyderabad (20%), Mumbai (66.0%), and Pune (44.0%) supported the same.

Another set of individuals believed that there wasn't any cultural difference which would cause them any security threat. That could be seen via responses across the six metro cities: Chennai (46.0%), Bengaluru (34.0%), Delhi (40.0%), Hyderabad (%), Mumbai (28.0%), and Pune (38.0%).

Figure 3.4 represents a graphical view of the total percentage of the responses by general population residing in six metro cities. The responses show that the general population across the six cities also believed that cultural difference was also one of the security threats to the Northeast people residing across the six metro cities.

Table 3.4 Responses of the general public related to security concerns residing in all six metropolitan cities

Prejudice		N	Percentage
Cultural difference, the major problem in Bangalore	0	7	14.0
	Cultural difference	26	52.0
	No cultural difference	17	34.0
Cultural difference, the major problem in Chennai	0	3	6.0
	Cultural difference	24	48.0
	No cultural difference	23	46.0
Cultural difference, the major problem in Delhi	0	1	2.0
	Cultural difference	29	58.0
	No cultural difference	20	40.0
Cultural difference, the major problem in Hyderabad	0	4	8.0
	Cultural difference	10	20.0
	No cultural difference	36	72.0
Cultural difference, the major problem in Mumbai	0	3	6.0
	Cultural difference	33	66.0
	No cultural difference	14	28.0
Cultural difference, the major problem in Pune	0	9	18.0
	Cultural difference	22	44.0
	No cultural difference	19	38.0
	Total	300	100.0

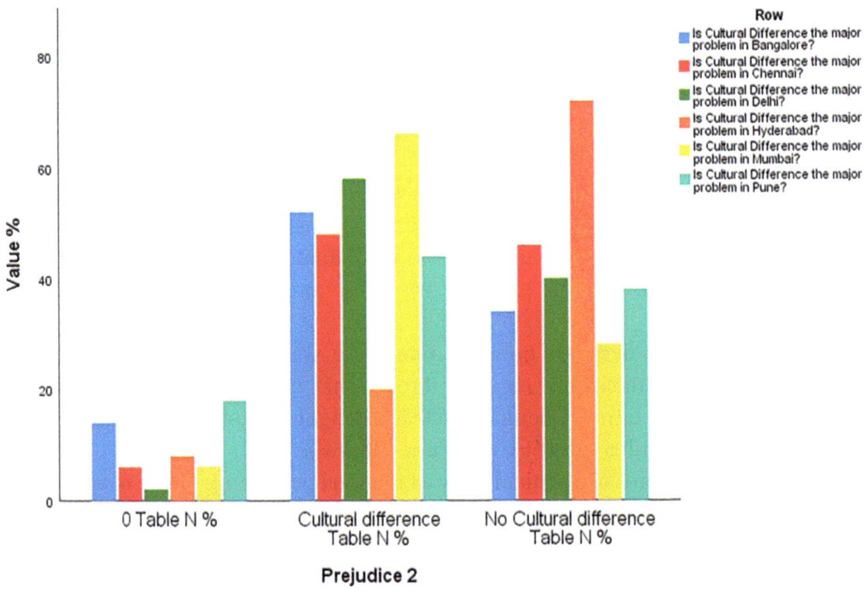

Fig. 3.4 Prejudice 2

3.1.2.2 Interpretation

It could be clearly observed from the data given in the above table that there was a variation in the responses obtained from different states. The aforementioned data were a representation of the general public and their responses with regard to cultural differences being the reason behind hate crime incidents against the Northeast Indians in metro cities. These responses depicted viewpoint of those people who were not at the epicenter of the hate crimes. Most general population in Mumbai responded in agreement that cultural differences between the people was one of the reasons behind hate crimes in the city, whereas most general people in Hyderabad agreed with the same stand.

3.1.3 Prejudice of Physical Appearance

In case of the second prejudice, i.e., *physical appearance*, the following responses were recorded.

Table 3.5 represents the total number of the Northeast populations that expressed whether they believed that prejudices like physical appearance act as a security concern across all six metro cities. Within the population of the Northeast people

Table 3.5 Responses of Northeastern people related to security concerns residing in all six metropolitan cities

Prejudice		N	Percentage
Physical appearance as the reason in Bangalore	0	40	26.7
	Physical appearance	75	50.0
	No physical appearance	35	23.3
Physical appearance as the reason in Chennai	0	29	19.3
	Physical appearance	102	68.0
	No physical appearance	19	12.7
Physical appearance as the reason in Delhi	0	38	25.3
	Physical appearance	77	51.3
	No physical appearance	35	23.3
Physical appearance as the reason in Hyderabad	0	52	34.7
	Physical appearance	65	43.3
	No physical appearance	33	22.0
Physical appearance as the reason in Mumbai	0	28	18.7
	Physical appearance	81	54.0
	No physical appearance	41	27.3
Physical appearance as the reason in Pune	0	48	32.0
	Physical appearance	68	45.3
	No physical appearance	34	22.7
	Total	900	100.0

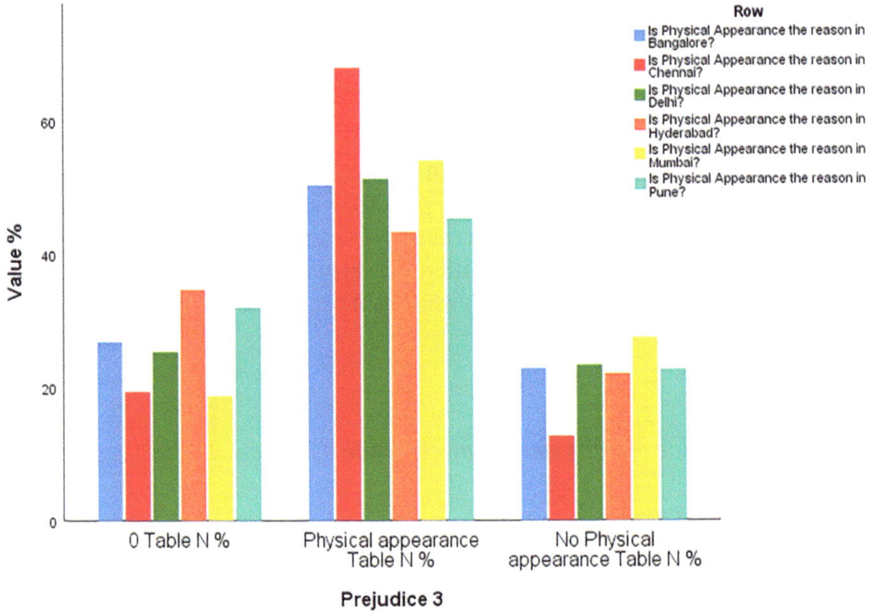

Fig. 3.5 Prejudice 3

residing across all six cities, there was a set of individuals who did not comment: Bengaluru (26.7%), Chennai (19.3%), Delhi 25.3 (%), Hyderabad (34.7%), Mumbai (18.7%), and Pune (32.0%).

However, there were individuals within the Northeast population who believed that physical appearance was leading to security threat against the Northeast people residing in the six metro cities. Around (68.0%) in Chennai, Bengaluru (50.0%), Delhi (51.3%), Hyderabad (43.3%), Mumbai (54.0%), and Pune (45.3%) supported the same. Another set of individuals believed that physical appearance would not cause them any security threat. That could be seen via responses across the six metro cities: Chennai (12.7%), Bengaluru (23.3%), Delhi (23.3%), Hyderabad (22.0%), Mumbai (27.3%), and Pune (22.7%).

Figure 3.5 represents a graphical view of the total percentage of the responses by Northeast people residing in six metro cities. The responses show that the Northeast population across the six cities largely believed that physical appearance was a security threat to them.

3.1.3.1 Interpretation

A higher percentage of Northeast Indian from metro cities believe that physical appearance was the reason for prejudice against them. More Northeast people in Chennai had the view that physical appearance remains one of the reasons which

Table 3.6 Responses of general public related to security concerns residing in all six metropolitan cities

Prejudice		N	Percentage
Physical appearance, the major problem in Bangalore	0	7	14.0
	Physical appearance	25	50.0
	Not physical appearance	18	36.0
Physical appearance, the major problem in Chennai	0	3	6.0
	Physical appearance	22	44.0
	No physical appearance	25	50.0
Physical appearance, the major problem in Delhi	0	1	2.0
	Physical appearance	38	76.0
	No physical appearance	11	22.0
Physical appearance, the major problem in Hyderabad	0	4	8.0
	Physical appearance	28	56.0
	No physical appearance	18	36.0
Physical appearance, the major problem in Mumbai	0	3	6.0
	Physical appearance	39	78.0
	No physical appearance	8	16.0
Physical appearance, the major problem in Pune	0	9	18.0
	Physical appearance	26	52.0
	No physical appearance	15	30.0
	Total	300	100.0

had led to hate crime incidents in the city, whereas most Northeast people in Mumbai believe that physical appearance between the people were not the primary reasons behind such crimes. That marked an identification to the fact that there was diversity in the Northeast population that was spread across the Indian subcontinent. The viewpoints of people differ in different cities and was thus visible in the data collected.

Table 3.6 represented the total number of general populations expressed whether they believed if prejudices like physical appearance acted as a security concern across all the six metro cities.

Within the population of the Northeast people residing across all six cities, there was a set of individuals who did not comment: Bengaluru (14%), Chennai (6%), Delhi (2%), Hyderabad (8%), Mumbai (6%), and Pune (18%).

However, there were individuals within the Northeast population who believed that physical appearance was leading to security threat against the general population residing in six metro cities. Around 44% in Chennai, 50% in Bengaluru, 76% in Delhi, 56% in Hyderabad, 78% in Mumbai, and 52% in Pune supported the same.

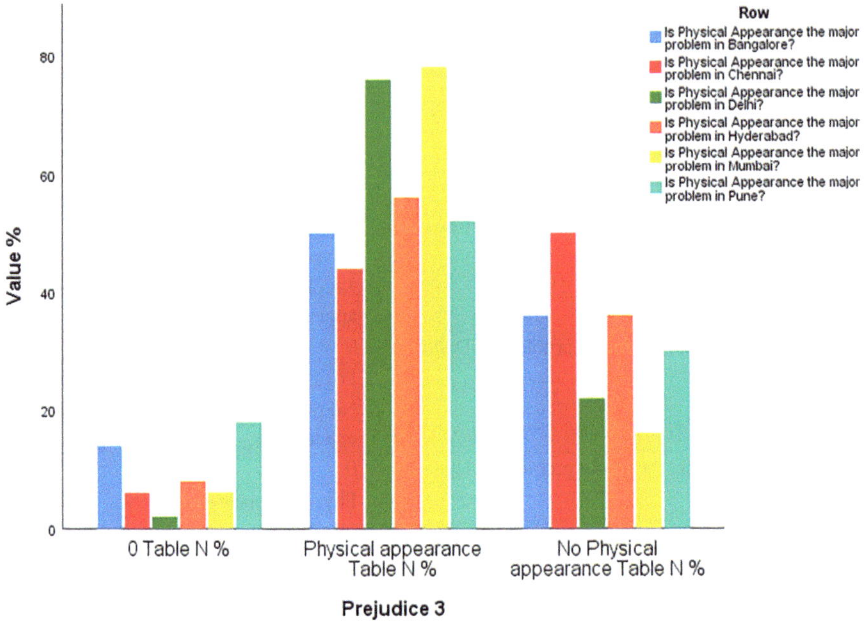

Fig. 3.6 Prejudice 3

Another set of individuals believed that there wasn't any circumstance that physical appearance would cause them any security threat. That could be seen via responses across the six metro cities: Chennai (50%), Bengaluru (36%), Delhi (22%), Hyderabad (36%), Mumbai (16%), and Pune (30%).

Figure 3.6 represents graphical view of the total percentage of the responses by general public residing in six metro cities. The responses showed that the general population across the six cities largely did not believe that physical appearance was a security threat to them.

3.1.3.2 Interpretation

In the present study, to gather data for hate crime incidents, it could be clearly observed from the above table that there was variation in the responses obtained in the different states. The aforementioned data was a representation of the general public and their responses with regards to physical appearance being the reason behind hate crime incidents against Northeast Indian in metro cities. These were responses which depicted from the viewpoint of those people who were not at the epicenter of the hate crimes. Most general population in Mumbai responded in agreement that physical appearance between the people was one of the reasons behind hate crimes in the city, and most general people in both Hyderabad and Bangalore agreed with the same stand.

3.2 Hypothesis Testing

Advanced statistical analysis of $_{Hn01}$ *= geographical indifference, physical appearance, and cultural difference had led to increase in prejudicial attitude against Northeast people residing in metro cities.*

Researchers performed Chi-square tests with regard to the three types of prejudices prevalent in the six metropolitan cities of India. These tests were conducted vis-à-vis police treatment that the Northeasterners in India receive as a result of these same prejudices. When police treatment was tested in correlation with geographical difference as a prejudice in Pune, Mumbai, New Delhi, Bangalore, Chennai, and Hyderabad, the following was the *key result* (Box 3.1):

Box 3.1: Key Results of Chi-Square Test with Geographical Difference as the Prejudice

- The value of the test statistic was 6.363.
- The footnote for this statistic pertains to the expected cell N assumption (i.e., expected cell Ns were all greater than 5): In total, 9 cells had an expected N less than 5, so this assumption was not met.
- Because the test statistic was based on a 3 × 2 cross-tabulation table, the degrees of freedom (df) for the test statistic was:

$$df = (R-1)*(C-1) = (3-1)*(2-1) = 6$$

- The corresponding *p*-value of the test statistic was $p = 0.384$

The interpretation was very clear that since the p-value was greater than our chosen significance level ($\alpha = 0.05$), null hypothesis was not rejected. Rather, it was concluded that there was not enough evidence to suggest an association between geographical indifference and police treatment in handling Northeast people suffering any kind of violence (Box 3.2).

Box 3.2: Key Results of Chi-Square Test with Cultural Difference as the Prejudice

- The value of the test statistic was 3.897.
- The footnote for this statistic pertains to the expected cell N assumption (i.e., expected cell Ns were all greater than 5): In total, 9 cells had an expected N less than 5, so this assumption was not met.
- Because the test statistic was based on a 3 × 2 cross-tabulation table, the degrees of freedom (df) for the test statistic was:

$$df = (R-1)*(C-1) = (3-1)*(2-1) = 6$$

- The corresponding *p*-value of the test statistic was $p = 0.691$

After analyzing geographical difference, we took cultural differences as the prejudice to test against police treatment in order to find out whether there was a correlation between the two.

What we can interpret from this was that since the p-value was greater than our chosen significance level ($\alpha = 0.05$), we do not reject the null hypothesis. Rather, we conclude that there was not enough evidence to suggest an association between cultural difference and police treatment in handling Northeast people suffering any kind of violence.

Table 3.7 Chi-square tests on all six cities related to prejudice (physical appearance)

Which metro city were you residing in?		Value	df	Asymptotic significance (2-sided)
Pune	Pearson Chi-square	2.643[a]	6	.001
	Likelihood ratio	20.878	6	.000
	Linear-by-linear association	10.716	1	.000
	N of valid cases	150		
Mumbai	Pearson Chi-square	2.407[b]	6	.000
	likelihood ratio	23.430	6	.000
	Linear-by-linear association	11.865	1	.000
	N of valid cases	150		
New Delhi	Pearson Chi-square	2.055[c]	6	.002
	Likelihood ratio	23.857	6	.000
	Linear-by-linear association	10.013	1	.000
	N of valid cases	150		
Bangalore	Pearson Chi-square	2.703[d]	6	.001
	Likelihood ratio	25.883	6	.000
	Linear-by-linear association	10.736	1	.000
	N of valid cases	150		
Chennai	Pearson Chi-square	2.268[e]	6	.000
	Likelihood ratio	22.990	6	.000
	Linear-by-linear association	11.993	1	.000
	N of valid cases	150		
Hyderabad	Pearson Chi-square	2.709[f]	6	.002
	Likelihood ratio	23.127	6	.000
	Linear-by-linear association	11.306	1	.000
	N of valid cases	150		
Total	Pearson Chi-square	1.938[g]	6	.001
	Likelihood r	13.203	6	.000
	Linear-by-linear association	66.247	1	.000
	N of valid cases	900		

[a]3 cells (25.0%) had expected N less than 5. The minimum expected N was 2.60
[b]2 cells (16.7%) had expected N less than 5. The minimum expected N was 2.24
[c]1 cell (8.3%) had expected N less than 5. The minimum expected N was 4.80
[d]2 cells (16.7%) had expected N less than 5. The minimum expected N was 2.90
[e]2 cells (16.7%) had expected N less than 5. The minimum expected N was 4.17
[f]2 cells (16.7%) had expected N less than 5. The minimum expected N was 2.64
[g]0 cells (0.0%) had expected N less than 5. The minimum expected N was 24.72

For the next part, physical appearance as the prejudice was taken to be correlated with police treatment that the Northeasterners get in India. The same is elaborated below:

The key result in the Chi-Square Tests Table 3.7 *was* (Box 3.3)*:*

Box 3.3: Key Results of Chi-Square Test with Physical Appearance as the Prejudice

- The value of the test statistic was 1.938.
- The footnote for this statistic pertains to the expected cell N assumption (i.e., expected cell Ns were all greater than 5): In total, 2 cells had an expected N less than 5, so this assumption was not met.
- Because the test statistic was based on a 3 × 2 cross-tabulation table, the degrees of freedom (df) for the test statistic was

$$df = (R-1)*(C-1) = (3-1)*(2-1) = 6$$

- The corresponding *p*-value of the test statistic was $p = 0.001$.

Since the *p*-value was less than our chosen significance level ($\alpha = 0.05$), we accept the null hypothesis. Rather, we conclude that there was enough evidence to suggest an association between physical appearance and police treatment in handling Northeast people suffering any kind of violence.

3.3 Awareness of Hate Crime

In this part, the researchers tried to understand the awareness quotient among Northeast people residing in all six cities.

The data collected represent the total number of Northeast populations on awareness related to hate crime across all six metro cities. Within the population of Northeast people residing across all six cities, there was a set of individuals who did not comment: Bengaluru (0.7%), Chennai (0.7%), Delhi (0.7%), Hyderabad (0.7%), Mumbai (1.3%), and Pune (3.3%).

However, there were individuals within the Northeast population who were aware about hate crime: Chennai (64.0%)i, Bengaluru (51.3%), Delhi (82.7%), Hyderabad (74.0%), Mumbai (88.0%), Pune (68.0%). Another set of individuals who weren't aware about this crime across six metro cities were as follows: Chennai (35.3%), Bengaluru (48.0%), Delhi (17.3%), Hyderabad (25.3%), Mumbai (10.7%), and Pune (28.7%). Second Fig. 3.5 represents graphical view of the total percentage of the responses by Northeast people residing in the six metro cities.

The responses showed that the Northeast population residing in Mumbai (88%) followed by Delhi (82.7%) were largely aware about the hate crime.

After assessing responses of the Northeast Indian population residing metropolitan cities, the study went further into understanding the general population responses regarding awareness related to hate crime across all six metro cities. Within the general population residing across all six cities, there were 6% individuals who did not comment on the issue. However, there were individuals within the general population who were aware about hate crime: Chennai (68%), Bengaluru (52%), Delhi (76%), Hyderabad (54%), Mumbai (82%), Pune (56%). Another set of individuals who weren't aware about this crime across six metro cities were as follows: Chennai (32%), Bengaluru (48%), Delhi (76%), Hyderabad (54%), Mumbai (82%), and Pune (56%).

The responses showed that the general population residing in Mumbai (82.0%), followed by Delhi (76.0%), was largely aware about hate crime.

3.4 N-E People Encountering Hate Crime Incidents

Table 3.8 and Fig. 3.7 represented the total number of incidences related to hate crime across all six metro cities against Northeast population. Within the Northeast population residing across all six cities, there were 17.3% individuals who did not comment on the issue. However, there were individuals within the Northeast who had encountered hate crime incidences: Chennai (35.3%), Bengaluru (32.7%),

Table 3.8 Northeast people encountering hate crime incidents

Encountered hate crime		N	Percentage
People encountered hate crime incident in Bangalore	0	65	43.3
	Yes	49	32.7
	No	36	24.0
People encountered hate crime incident in Chennai	0	45	30.0
	Yes	53	35.3
	No	52	34.7
People encountered hate crime incident in Delhi	0	11	7.3
	Yes	65	43.3
	No	74	49.3
People encountered hate crime incident in Hyderabad	0	21	14.0
	Yes	37	24.7
	No	92	61.3
People encountered hate crime incident in Mumbai	0	14	9.3
	Yes	67	44.7
	No	69	46.0
People encountered hate crime incident in Pune	0	26	17.3
	Yes	48	32.0
	No	76	50.7
	Total	900	100.0

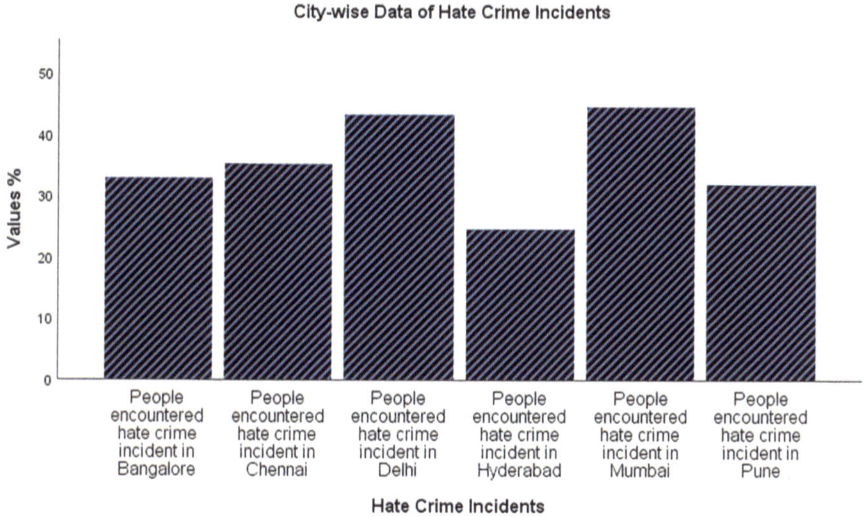

Fig. 3.7 Hate crime incidents

Delhi (43.3%), Hyderabad (24.7%), Mumbai (44.7%), and Pune (32.0%). Another set of individuals who did not encounter hate crime were: Chennai (34.7%), Bengaluru (24.0%), Delhi (49.3%), Hyderabad (61.3%), Mumbai (46.0%), and Pune (50.7%).

Figure 3.7 represents a graphical view of the total percentage of the responses by people residing in six metro cities. The responses showed that the Northeast population residing in Mumbai (44.7%), followed by Delhi (43.3%), largely encountered hate crime incidences.

3.5 N-E People Witnessing Hate Crime Incidents

Table 3.9 and Fig. 3.8 represent the total number of Northeast people witnessing Hate Crime incidences across all six metro cities. Within the Northeast population residing across all six cities there were 12.7% individuals who did not comment on the issue. However, there were individuals within the Northeast who had witnessed hate crime incidences: Chennai (66%), Bengaluru (40%), Delhi (59.3%), Hyderabad (46%), Mumbai (64.7%), and Pune (54.7%). Another set of individuals who did not witness hate crime incidences were: Chennai (32.7%), Bengaluru (52%), Delhi (32.7%), Hyderabad (43.3%), Mumbai (30%), and Pune (32.7%).

Figure 3.8 represents graphical view of the total percentage of the responses by people residing in six metro cities. The responses showed that the Northeast population residing in Chennai (66%), followed by Mumbai (64.7%), largely witnessed hate crime incidences.

Table 3.9 Northeast people witnessing hate crime incidents

Witnessing hate crime		N	Percentage
People witnessed hate crime incident in Bangalore	0	12	8.0
	Yes	60	40.0
	No	78	52.0
People witnessed hate crime incident in Chennai	0	2	1.3
	Yes	99	66.0
	No	49	32.7
People witnessed hate crime incident in Delhi	0	12	8.0
	Yes	89	59.3
	No	49	32.7
People witnessed hate crime incident in Hyderabad	0	16	10.7
	Yes	69	46.0
	No	65	43.3
People witnessed hate crime incident in Mumbai	0	8	5.3
	Yes	97	64.7
	No	45	30.0
People witnessed hate crime incident in Pune	0	19	12.7
	Yes	82	54.7
	No	49	32.7
	Total	900	100.0

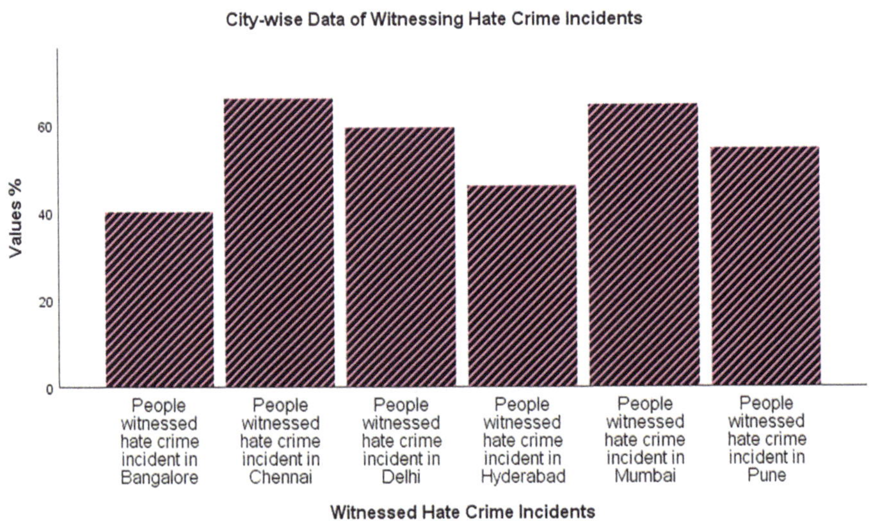

Fig. 3.8 Witnessing hate crime

3.6 People Known to General Population Encountering/Witnessing Hate Crime

This data represented the general population witnessing/encountering hate crime incidences against Northeast people known to them, across all six metro cities. Within the population residing across all six cities, 6% of the individuals from Pune, 10% from Delhi, 4% from Hyderabad, 6% from Mumbai, and 36% from Pune did not comment on the issue.

However, there were individuals within the respondents who had witnessed/encountered hate crime incidences committed against known Northeast people like in Chennai (20%), Bengaluru (14%), Delhi (66%), Hyderabad (38%), Mumbai (22%), and Pune (10%). Another set of individuals who did not encounter hate crime incidences against known Northeast people were: Chennai (80%), Bengaluru (80%), Delhi (24%), Hyderabad (58%), Mumbai (72%), and Pune (54%).

The responses showed that the Northeast population residing in Delhi (66%) followed by Hyderabad (38%) largely encountered hate crime incidences against known Northeast people, as witnessed by the general population respondents.

3.6.1 Interpretation

In the above data presented, responses had been collected from the general population in order to understand how this crime was seen from another's point of view. People committing such hate crimes belong to this group of general population so it becomes important that their perceptions and viewpoints were recorded along with the Northeast population in these six metro cities. From the above data, it could be seen that mostly respondents from Delhi had witnessed/encountered hate crime incidents being committed against Northeast Indian people known to them, whereas the least number of respondents from Chennai and Bengaluru had encountered such crimes committed against Northeast Indians. Witnessing a hate crime or encountering a hate crime is used together or sometimes interchangeably for the general population because these data were merged together in order to subtly signify the hate crime incidents which the general population of these cities themselves have witnessed or encountered among the Northeastern Indians they know.

3.7 Types of Hate Crime Committed

In this segment, data were collected to depict the ways by which hate crimes were committed against Northeast Indians in six different cities. Northeastern respondents were asked from six metro cities of India – Bangalore, Chennai, Delhi, Hyderabad, Mumbai, and Pune (Box 3.4).

Box 3.4: Types of Hate Crime Committed

The study conducted in this book discussed few types of hate crimes that were conducted against Northeast Indians in metro cities. They are:

1. Offensive and abusive language
2. Coercive and threatening behavior
3. Mediated threats
4. Physical assault
5. Sexual remarks
6. Sexual assault
7. Material criminal damage
8. Incitement

It was seen that in Bangalore, 43.3% respondents faced offensive and abusive language, 26% faced coercive and threatening behavior, 10% faced mediated threats, 18% faced physical assault, 9.3% faced sexual remarks, 10.7% faced sexual assault, 15.3% faced material and criminal damage, and 5.3% faced incitement.

In Chennai, 72% of the respondents faced offensive and abusive language, 36.7% faced coercive and threatening behavior, 4.7% faced mediated threats, 23.3% faced physical assault, 22.7% faced sexual remarks, 10.7% faced sexual assault, 34% faced material and criminal damage, and 4% faced incitement.

In Delhi, 64% of the respondents faced offensive and abusive language, 22% faced coercive and threatening behavior, 7.3% faced mediated threats, 12% faced physical assault, 19.3% faced sexual remarks, 7.3% faced sexual assault, 1.3% faced material and criminal damage, and 13.3% faced incitement.

In Hyderabad, 48.7% of the respondents faced offensive and abusive language, 10.7% faced coercive and threatening behavior, 1.3% faced mediated threats, 8% faced physical assault, 13.3% faced sexual remarks, 4.7% faced sexual assault, 2.7% faced material and criminal damage, and 5.3% faced incitement.

In Mumbai, 74% respondents faced offensive and abusive language, 8% faced coercive and threatening behavior, 21.3% faced mediated threats, 18% faced physical assault, 13.3% faced sexual remarks, 9.3% faced sexual assault, 7.3% faced material and criminal damage, and 6% faced incitement.

In Pune, 67.3% respondents faced offensive and abusive language, 17.3% faced coercive and threatening behavior, 2% faced mediated threats, 13.3% faced physical assault, 12.7% faced sexual remarks, 4.7% faced sexual assault, 4.7% faced material and criminal damage, and 2.7% faced incitement.

3.7.1 Interpretation

The data depicted the information regarding types of hate crimes that were committed against the Northeast Indians in six different cities. This means to say, it enumerates eight kinds of ways by which this crime was committed and the number of the respondents that had faced from the sample of the Northeast population taken.

It was pertinent to note that in Bangalore, hate crime by way of offensive and abusive language against the Northeast Indian people were committed the most, i.e., 43.3% of the respondents, and incitement against the Northeast Indian people were committed the least, i.e., 5.3% of the respondents.

In Chennai, hate crime by way of offensive and abusive language against the Northeast Indian people were committed the most, i.e., 72% of the respondents, and incitement against the Northeast Indian people were committed the least, i.e., 4% of the respondents.

In Delhi, hate crime by way of offensive and abusive language against the Northeast Indian people were committed the most, i.e., 64% of the respondents, and material and criminal damage against the Northeast Indian people were committed the least, i.e., 1.3% of the respondents.

In Hyderabad, hate crime by way of offensive and abusive language against the Northeast Indian people were committed the most, i.e., 48.7% of the respondents, and mediated threat against Northeast Indian people were committed the least, i.e., 1.3% of the respondents.

In Mumbai, hate crime by way of offensive and abusive language against the Northeast Indian people were committed the most, i.e., 74% of the respondents, and incitement against the Northeast Indian people were committed the least, i.e., 6% of the respondents.

In Pune, hate crime by way of offensive and abusive language against the Northeast Indian people were committed the most, i.e., 67.3% of the respondents, and mediated threat against the Northeast Indian people were committed the least, i.e., 2% of the respondents.

From the above, we could observe that hate crime by way of offensive and abusive language against Northeast Indian people in metro cities were committed in the greatest degree. Calling offensively and name-calling are common practices that the Northeastern folk in metro cities suffer from. Throughout the study, this account is a common experience shared by all the Northeastern respondents.

3.8 Location of Experiencing Hate Crimes

To appropriately map the place where hate crime incidents against Northeasterners take place, data had been accumulated depicting hate crime experience of the Northeast population in six metro cities in India.

In Bangalore, 2.7% of the respondents had suffered from hate crime in schools, 10.7% had suffered in college, 6% in workplace, 11.3% in public places, and 9.3% in public transport.

In Chennai, 0% of the respondents had suffered from hate crime in schools, 8% had suffered in college, 0.7% in workplace, 9.3% in public places, and 4% in public transport.

In Delhi, 2% of the respondents had suffered from hate crime in schools, 8.7% had suffered in college, 1.3% in workplace, 34.7% in public places, and 4% in public transport.

In Hyderabad, 2% of the respondents had suffered from hate crime in schools, 4.7% had suffered in college, 2% in workplace, 11.3% in public places, and 4% in public transport.

In Mumbai, 2.7% of the respondents had suffered from hate crime in schools, 5.3% had suffered in college, 4.7% in workplace, 16% in public places, and 3.3% in public transport.

In Pune, 0.7% of the respondents had suffered from hate crime in schools, 3.3% had suffered in college, 3.3% in workplace, 12.7% in public places, and 4.7% in public transport.

3.8.1 Interpretation

From the above data, it could be observed that in most incidents of hate crimes, Northeast Indians had experienced the crime in public places in all the six metro cities of Bangalore, Chennai, Delhi, Hyderabad, Mumbai, and Pune. The least experiences had been gathered from schools. This was unfortunate to mention that incidents of hate crimes mostly were seen to have taken place in public places. Consequences are manifold since the humiliation that the Northeast people have suffer from in a public place has an extremely long-lasting effect in their minds, and also the rest of the public who witness such crimes may or may not imbibe the same actions in treating the Northeast Indians. It was necessary that such facts were also considered while analyzing the hate crime incidents against the Northeast Indians residing in metro cities.

3.9 Major Problems Behind Hate Crimes

In this section, the study depicted the major problems which may had been the cause of hate crime incidents in the respective metro cities. The statistics highlight those problems that exist according to the Northeast Indians living in those cities that had led to the commission of hate crimes.

In Bangalore, 5.4% of the Northeastern respondents believe that different physical appearance and ethnicity was the major problem behind hate crime incidents,

17.4% of the Northeastern respondents believe public attitude and their insensitivity to be the major problem, 4% believe Northeastern people were not considered Indian citizens and that this difference causes the crime, 8.1% responded that it's the lack of awareness and knowledge about issues of hate crimes, and 3.3% perceive that nonrecognition of hate crimes was the major reason behind hate crimes against the Northeast Indians in metro cities.

In Chennai, 13.3% of the Northeast respondents believe that different physical appearance and ethnicity was the major problem behind hate crime incidents, 11.3% of the Northeast respondents believe public attitude and their insensitivity to be the major problem, 2% believe Northeast people were not considered Indian citizens and that this difference causes the crime, 21.3% responded that it's lack of awareness and knowledge about issues of hate crimes, and 5.3% perceive nonrecognition of hate crimes the major reason behind hate crimes against the Northeast Indians in metro cities.

In Delhi, 17.3% of the Northeast respondents believe that different physical appearance and ethnicity was the major problem behind hate crime incidents, 24% of the Northeastern respondents believe public attitude and their insensitivity to be the major problem, 4.7% believe Northeast people were not considered Indian citizens and that this difference causes the crime, 14.7% responded that it's lack of awareness and knowledge about issues of hate crimes, and 4.7% perceive nonrecognition of hate crimes the major reason behind hate crimes against the Northeast Indians in metro cities.

In Hyderabad, 9.3% of the Northeast respondents believe that different physical appearance and ethnicity was the major problem behind hate crime incidents, 12.7% of the Northeast respondents believe public attitude and their insensitivity to be the major problem, 2.7% believe Northeast people were not considered Indian citizens and that this difference causes the crime, 11.3% responded that it's lack of awareness and knowledge about issues of hate crimes, and 2% perceive nonrecognition of hate crimes the major reason behind hate crimes against the Northeast Indians in metro cities.

In Mumbai, 18.7% of the Northeastern respondents believe that different physical appearance and ethnicity was the major problem behind hate crime incidents, 14% of the Northeastern respondents believe public attitude and their insensitivity to be the major problem, 3.3% believe Northeastern people were not considered Indian citizens and that this difference causes the crime, 17.3% responded that it's lack of awareness and knowledge about issues of hate crimes, and 2.7% perceive nonrecognition of hate crimes the major reason behind hate crimes against the Northeast Indians in metro cities.

In Pune, 11.3% of the Northeastern respondents believe that different physical appearance and ethnicity was the major problem behind hate crime incidents, 2.7% of the Northeastern respondents believe public attitude and their insensitivity to be the major problem, 3.3% believe Northeastern people were not considered Indian citizens and that this difference causes the crime, 8% responded that it's lack of awareness and knowledge about issues of hate crime, and 3.3% perceive nonrecognition of hate crimes the major reason behind hate crimes against the Northeast Indians in metro cities.

3.9.1 Interpretation

From the above data, it could be clearly observed that there were five reasons that people had limited their responses to. The coding according to the responses was done after accumulating perceptions of the Northeast people for this part of the research. According to the responses, most people in Bangalore believed public attitude and their insensitivity to be the major problem; in Chennai, most respondents believed lack of awareness and knowledge about the issues of hate crime was the major problem; in Delhi, most respondents believed public attitude and insensitivity was the major problem; in Hyderabad, most respondents believed public attitude and their insensitivity was the major problem; in Mumbai, most respondents believed their own physical appearance and ethnicity was the major problem; and in Pune, most respondents believed their own physical appearance and ethnicity was the major problem.

3.10 Mental Status of Victims of Hate Crime

In the next segment, the study emphasized on the mental status of the Northeastern people during commission of hate crime incident in metro cities. The purpose was to understand what kind of mental impact these acts have, in addition to the physical acts.

In Bangalore, 16.7% of the Northeast Indians felt afraid and unsafe during the commission of the incident, 6% of the respondents were uncomfortable and humiliated, 2% of the Northeasterners felt conscious about their physical appearance and identity, and 2% of the respondents were angry and vengeful while being the victim of the hate crime incident.

In Chennai, 14.7% of the Northeast Indians felt afraid and unsafe during the commission of the incident, 8% of the respondents were uncomfortable and humiliated, 1.3% of the Northeasterners felt conscious about their physical appearance and identity, and 3.3% of the respondents were angry and vengeful while being the victim of the hate crime incident.

In Delhi, 17.3% of the Northeast Indians felt afraid and unsafe during the commission of the incident, 9.3% of the respondents were uncomfortable and humiliated, 0% of the Northeasterners felt conscious about their physical appearance and identity, and 0.7% of the respondents were angry and vengeful while being the victim of the hate crime incident.

In Hyderabad, 7.3% of the Northeast Indians felt afraid and unsafe during the commission of the incident, 1.3% of the respondents were uncomfortable and humiliated, 2% of the Northeasterners felt conscious about their physical appearance and identity, and 1.3% of the respondents were angry and vengeful while being the victim of the hate crime incident.

In Mumbai, 8.7% of the Northeast Indians felt afraid and unsafe during the commission of the incident, 7.3% of the respondents were uncomfortable and humiliated, 6% of the Northeasterners felt conscious about their physical appearance and identity, and 4.7% of the respondents were angry and vengeful while being the victim of the hate crime incident.

In Pune, 8.7% of the Northeast Indians felt afraid and unsafe during the commission of the incident, 2.7% of the respondents were uncomfortable and humiliated, 1.3% of the Northeasterners felt conscious about their physical appearance and identity, and 2% of the respondents were angry and vengeful while being the victim of the hate crime incident.

3.10.1 Interpretation

It could be seen from the data above that mostly Northeast Indian respondents felt afraid and unsafe during the commission of the incident of hate crime. Delhi was the metropolitan city, followed by Bangalore, that had most such responses given by the Northeasterners. This could be concluded by the researchers that mental harassment and torture that was faced by these victims were far greater than the physical injury attained. The fear felt by the victims follow these people even after the incident had passed. This remains to be a kind of trauma upon the Northeast people during the commission of hate crime and thus becomes imperative to be dealt with.

3.11 Possible Perpetrators Reported

In the last study for this chapter, data showcased is about the possible perpetrators of hate crimes as reported by the Northeastern people in metro cities.

In Bangalore, it was reported that around 6.6% of landlords made certain comments or were not welcoming, 78% of the strangers made certain remarks which was the highest number, 13.5% of friends/acquaintances passed comments or were indulged into certain unacceptable behavior, 30% of neighbors, people at workplace were reported to be at 3%, and at the university/college level, 52.5%; however, 33% chose to remain silent.

In Chennai, 30% of the Northeastern population reported landlords to be possible perpetrators, and around 7.5% were neighbors, 15% were friends/acquaintances, strangers were at 67.5% (maximum), people at workplace were reported to be at 28.5%, and at the university/college level, 45%; however, 43.5% chose to remain silent.

In Delhi, 4.5% of landlords were reported to be possible perpetrators, and around 22.5% were neighbors, 16.5% were friends/acquaintances, strangers were at 49.5% (maximum), people at workplace were reported to be at 45%, and at the university/college level, 27%; however, 60% chose to remain silent.

In Hyderabad, it was reported that around 15% of landlords made certain comments or were not welcoming, 51% of the strangers made certain remarks which was the highest number, 30% of friends/acquaintances passed comments or were indulged into certain unacceptable behavior, neighbors were at 15%, people at workplace were reported to be at 6%, and at the university/college level, 36%; however, 72% chose to remain silent.

In Mumbai, it was reported that around 15% of landlords made certain comments or were not welcoming, 42% of the strangers made certain remarks which was the highest number,

3% of friends/acquaintances passed comments or were indulged into certain unacceptable behavior, neighbors were at 10.5%, people at workplace were reported to be at 7.5%, and 15% at the university/college level; however, 132% chose to remain silent.

In Pune, it was reported that around 4.5% of landlords made certain comments or were not welcoming, 16.5% of the strangers made certain remarks, 27% of friends/acquaintances passed comments or were indulged into certain unacceptable behavior, neighbors were at 12%, people at workplace were reported to be at 10.5%, and 7.5% at the university/college level; however, 11.5% chose to remain silent.

3.11.1 Interpretation

It could be seen from the data above that the highest percentage of the possible perpetrators reported by the Northeast population was of strangers across all the cities. However, in Pune City, it was seen that friends/acquaintances were reported to be of higher percentage. It was noted that out of the six cities, four reported strangers to be possible perpetrators of hate crime incidences. Maximum of the population chose to remain silent or avoided to share such information (Box 3.5).

Box 3.5: Important Note

It is also to be noted that in every dataset taken in this book, $n = 150$ across six cities. In total (all six cities); $n = 900$ as the researchers had merged the data together for better representation and understanding. The percentage representation was done keeping $n = 150$.

Chapter 4
Secondary Victimization During Post-victimization Stages

4.1 Introduction

This chapter had tried to bring forth the various consequences associated with the hate crime post the incident. The chapter mentions various agencies approached by the Northeast population for reporting of the incident and the approach taken by the agencies after reporting of the incidences in respect to the hate crimes across six metro cities.

The research team had also studied how much of a success the investigation process was after the incidence was reported. The concept of secondary victimization enhances the in-depth knowledge about the consequences associated with hate crime.

The second half of the section further deals with the testing of the hypothesis ($_{Hn02}$) mentioned in Chap. 1 and also helped to develop an understanding as to whether dearth of legal protection had led to increase in hate crime incidents against Northeast population. The advanced statistical analysis was done so that the interaction of various variables could be ascertained. The data of both the target groups was taken into account, i.e., of the Northeast and general population residing in the six metro cities.

4.2 After-Effects of Hate Crime Incident

Figure 4.1 showcased the after-effects of the hate crime that the Northeast Indian respondents had suffered. These consequences or the various types of after-effects that the Northeastern people went through were statistically bifurcated among six metro cities. Broadly speaking, the consequences of hate crime incident include avoiding going out at night, avoiding going to places where one experienced the hate crime, starting to go out at certain time of the day which the victim considered

G. S. Bajpai et al., *Hate Crime in India*,
https://doi.org/10.1007/978-3-031-30522-1_4

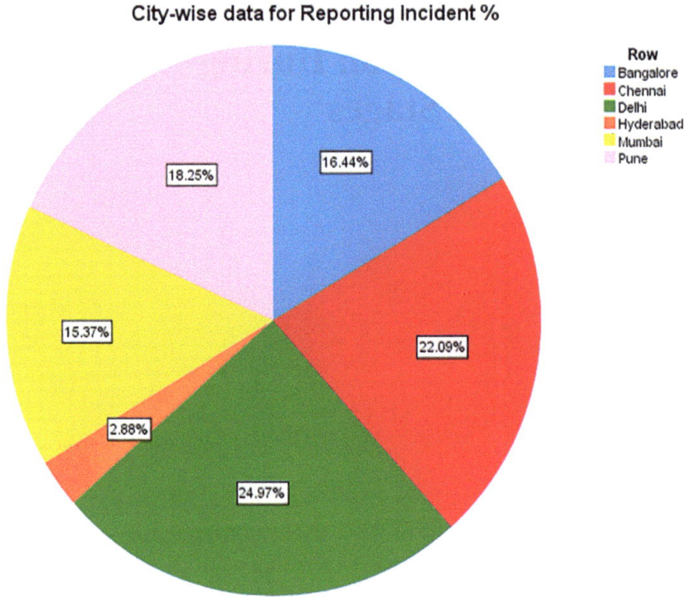

Fig. 4.1 Metro city-wise tabulation of after-effects of incident

safe, changing their schedule, stopped going out alone, retaliating against it, or avoiding the situation altogether. In the data, there were such respondents who did not feel comfortable answering the question, and they were symbolized by the value 0.

A total of 21.3% Northeast Indians avoided going at night, out of which the highest percentage of such people were in Mumbai with 4.6%; 20.8% Northeast Indians avoided going to places where they experienced the hate crime, out of which the highest percentage of such people were going out at certain time of the day which they considered safe, out of which the highest percentage of such people were in Chennai with 3.9%; 9.7% Northeast Indians changed their schedule, out of which the highest percentage of such people were in Chennai with 4.6%; 17.6% Northeast Indians stopped going out alone, out of which the highest percentage of such people were in Chennai with 5.1%; 5.3% Northeast Indians retaliated against the incident, out of which the highest percentage of such people were in New Delhi and Bangalore with 1.2%; and 32.2% Northeast Indians avoided the situation revolving around the incident, out of which the highest percentage of such people were in Chennai with 8.2%.

The total number of observations was 900 since n = 150 in one state, and there were six cities in total. Combined statistics of the cities, i.e., Pune, Mumbai, New Delhi, Bangalore, Chennai, and Hyderabad were taken into account in the Fig. 4.1.

4.2.1 Interpretation

We could observe from the combined statistics of the six metro cities that mostly Northeast Indian people chose avoiding the incident of hate crime, i.e., 32.2%, and most percentage of such people were from Chennai, i.e., 8.2% people. This means that even though Northeast people witnessed or encountered the incident of hate crimes in metro cities, they chose not to report about such an incident, but instead ignored the issue. This means that the Northeastern people felt letting go of the incident was the right choice and did not think reporting of the crime was appropriate in a law-abiding police-monitored society. There could be a number of reasons for such a response to the crime which would be dealt within the following segments.

4.3 Reporting Agency

This section of the chapter details which reporting agency was approached by both the Northeast Indians and general population people in cases where either the incidents were suffered by or witnessed, respectively. This becomes important in order to locate the agency that is most approachable and more effective in reaching the people in metropolitan cities in redressing hate crime incidents against the Northeasterners (Box 4.1).

Box 4.1: Reporting Agencies Mapped

1. Police
2. Educational organizations
3. Local councils
4. Social enterprises
5. Any other institution/organization

The data highlighted the percentage of the Northeast Indian people in metro cities who resorted to reporting the hate crime suffered by them to authorities like police, educational organizations, local councils, social enterprise, or any other institution. A total of 900 respondents were taken for the purpose of this data analyzation. In the data, there were such respondents who did not feel comfortable answering the question and were symbolized by the value 0.

In Bangalore, 6% of the Northeast people reported to the police, 4.7% reported to educational organizations, 1.3% reported to local councils, 4% reported to social enterprises, and 1.3% reported to any other organization.

In Chennai, 10% of the Northeast people reported to the police, 6.7% reported to educational organizations, 0% reported to local councils, 0% reported to social enterprises, and 2.7% reported to any other organization.

In Delhi, 4% of the Northeast people reported to the police, 7.3% reported to educational organizations, 0% reported to local councils, 0.7% reported to social enterprises, and 4.7% reported to any other organization.

In Hyderabad, 1.3% of the Northeast people reported to the police, 1.3% reported to educational organizations, 0% reported to local councils, 0% reported to social enterprises, and 1.3% reported to any other organization.

In Mumbai, 9.3% of the Northeast people reported to the police, 0% reported to educational organizations, 1.3% reported to local councils, 0% reported to social enterprises, and 3.3% reported to any other organization.

In Pune, 8.7% of the Northeast people reported to the police, 4% reported to educational organizations, 0% reported to local councils, 2% reported to social enterprises, and 2.7% reported to any other organization.

4.3.1 Interpretation

In Bangalore, Chennai, Mumbai, and Pune, most people resorted to reporting the matter to the police. In Delhi, people reported the incident mostly in educational institutions. In Hyderabad, people equally resorted to reporting the crime in educational institutions and the police. This indicates the scenario wherein victims of the crime had faith in the concerned organization for the purpose of redressal from hate crime.

In another part, the general population were also analyzed. It was to see that when subjected to hate crime incidents as a by-stander or an acquaintance of the person who suffered it, whether these people reported the incident to the concerned organization regarding the incident. A total of 300 respondents had been taken for the purpose of this data analyzation. In the data, there were such respondents who did not feel comfortable answering the question and were symbolized by the value 0.

In Bangalore, 2% of the general people reported to the police, 2% reported to educational organizations, 4% reported to local councils, 0% reported to social enterprises, 2% reported to more than one of the organizations mentioned above, and 0% reported to any other organization.

In Chennai, 2% of the general people reported to the police, 4% reported to educational organizations, 0% reported to local councils, 0% reported to social enterprises, and 4% reported to any other organization.

In Delhi, 12% of the general people reported to the police, 6% reported to educational organizations, 4% reported to local councils, 2% reported to social enterprises, and 2% reported to any other organization.

In Hyderabad, 16% of the general people reported to the police, 8% reported to educational organizations, 2% reported to local councils, 2% reported to social enterprises, and 0% reported to any other organization.

In Mumbai, 6% of the general people reported to the police, 6% reported to educational organizations, 2% reported to local councils, 0% reported to social enterprises, and 0% reported to any other organization.

In Pune, 2% of the general people reported to the police, 0% reported to educational organizations, 0% reported to local councils, 0% reported to social enterprises, and 6% reported to any other organization.

4.3.2 *Interpretation*

In Bangalore, most people resorted to reporting the crime to local councils. In Chennai, people reported mostly to educational institutions. In Delhi, Hyderabad, Mumbai, and Pune, people mostly resorted to reporting the hate crime incident to the police. This indicates that victims of the crime had faith n the concerned organization for the purpose of redressal of hate crimes.

4.4 Reporting of Incident

Data to be studied in any quantitative research regarding hate crime incidents would be futile if cases are left unreported. This segment highlights whether cases are being reported by the Northeast Indians or the general population people in the six metropolitan cities, i.e., Bangalore, Chennai, Pune, Mumbai, Hyderabad, and Delhi. This would also indicate how effectively redressal mechanisms are reaching the affected persons in the cities.

4.4.1 *Reporting of the Incident to Police by Northeast Indians*

Table 4.1 indicates a city-wise measure of the number of respondents who considered reporting of incident to the police as an appropriate response to the commission of the crime. A total of 900 respondents were taken for the purpose of this data analyzation. In the data, there were such respondents who did not feel comfortable answering the question and were symbolized by the value 0.

Table 4.1 Metro city-wise data on reporting of hate crime incident to the police by N-E population

	0		Yes		No		Total	
	N	Percentage	N	Percentage	N	Percentage	N	Percentage
Bangalore	13	8.7	17	11.4	120	79.9	150	100.0
Chennai	10	6.7	23	15.3	117	78.0	150	100.0
Delhi	21	14.0	26	17.3	103	68.7	150	100.0
Hyderabad	47	31.3	3	2.0	100	66.7	150	100.0
Mumbai	25	16.7	16	10.7	109	72.7	150	100.0
Pune	36	24.0	19	12.7	95	63.3	150	100.0

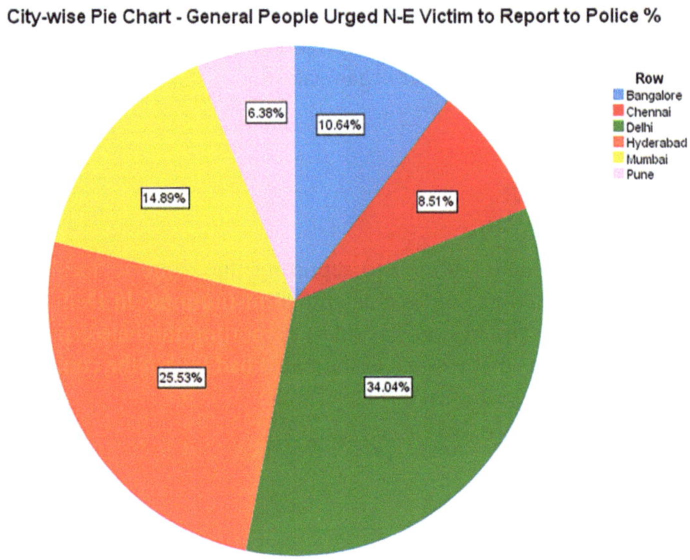

Fig. 4.2 Metro city-wise data on reporting of hate crime incident to the police by the Northeast people

Out of the total respondents of 150 from each of the six cities, 11.4% of the Northeast people suffering from hate crime incident from Bangalore reported the incident to the police, 15.3% from Chennai, 17.3% from Delhi, 2% from Hyderabad, and 10.7% from Mumbai, and 12.7% of the Northeast Indians reported the matter to the police. Whereas 79.9% of the Northeast Indian people in Bangalore believed that reporting the incident was not the right choice, 78% in Chennai, 68.7% in Delhi, 66.7% in Hyderabad, and 72.7% in Mumbai, 63.3% of the Northeast Indians in Pune did not resort to reporting the crime with the police.

Graphical representation of the percentage of the Northeast people reporting the incident to the police had been shown in the above Fig. 4.2.

4.4.1.1 Interpretation

After analyzing the above data, it was clear that the Northeast Indians from the metro city of Delhi were comparatively more supportive toward reporting the hate crime incident to the police. And mostly Northeast Indian people from Bangalore do not resort to reporting of the crime to the police. However, after an obtuse observance of the data, it cannot be overlooked that a greater number of the Northeast Indian people do not report the incident to the police. It was alarming to see that even after a history of procedural mechanisms in place for victims to seek remedy through, lesser number of people believe that reporting should be done in an incident concerning hate crime against the Northeast Indian people in metro cities.

4.4.2 *General People Advised Northeast Indians to Report the Incident to the Police*

Table 4.2 indicates a city-wise measure of the number of respondents who considered reporting of incident to the police as an appropriate response to the commission of the crime. In this segment, general people were interviewed who believed that in the event they either witnessed the hate crime incident as a bystander or encountered the incident with an acquaintance and asked whether they advised the victim of the crime to report the incident to the police.

A total of 300 respondents were taken for the purpose of this data analyzation. In the data, there were such respondents who did not feel comfortable answering the question and were symbolized by the value 0.

Out of the total respondents of 150 from each of the six states, 10% of the general people advised the Northeast victim suffering from hate crime incident from Bangalore to report the incident to the police, 8% from Chennai, 32% from Delhi, 24% from Hyderabad, and 14% from Mumbai, and 6% of the general population advised to report the matter to the police.

Whereas 12% of the general people in Bangalore believed that reporting the incident by the Northeast Indians was not the right choice, 14% in Chennai, 36% in Delhi, 18% in Hyderabad, and 14% in Mumbai, and 8% of the general population in Pune did not advise toward reporting the crime with the police. Graphical representation of the percentage of the Northeast people reporting the incident to the police has been shown in the below Fig. 4.3.

4.4.2.1 Interpretation

It could be observed from the above statistical data that comparing the two responses, the likelihood of general population advising the Northeast Indian victims of hate crime to report the incident to the police was grim. This means to say that the general population in the metro cities despite of witnessing or encountering such hate crime incidents do not consider reporting the matter to the police as the right choice in such a scenario.

Table 4.2 Metro city-wise data on reporting of hate crime incident to the police

General people advised to report to the police	0		Yes		No		Total	
	N	Percentage	N	Percentage	N	Percentage	N	Percentage
Bangalore	39	78.0	5	10.0	6	12.0	50	100.0
Chennai	39	78.0	4	8.0	7	14.0	50	100.0
Delhi	16	32.0	16	32.0	18	36.0	50	100.0
Hyderabad	29	58.0	12	24.0	9	18.0	50	100.0
Mumbai	36	72.0	7	14.0	7	14.0	50	100.0
Pune	43	86.0	3	6.0	4	8.0	50	100.0

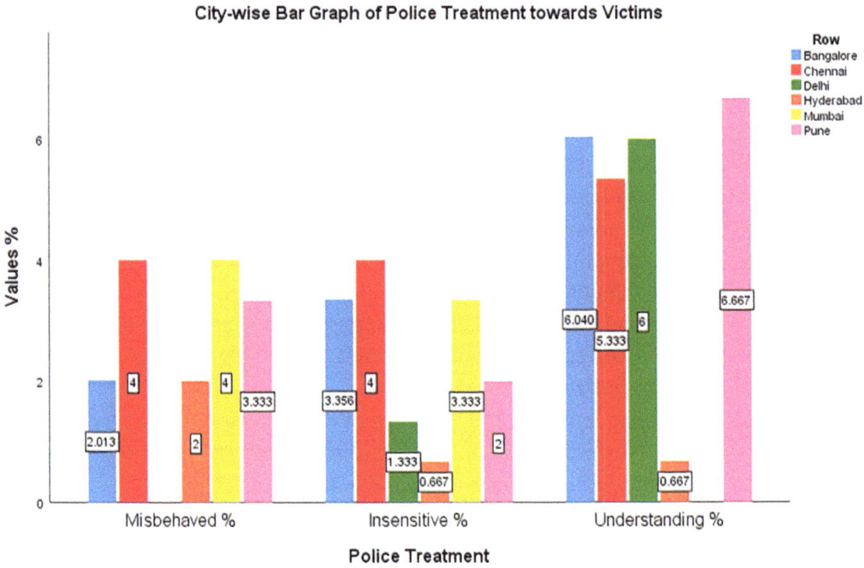

Fig. 4.3 Metro city-wise data on reporting of hate crime incident to the police by general people

The trends seen in the practice of reporting the matter to the police against the hate crime incidents against the Northeast Indian people was discouraging to witness. This was indicative of some other underlying gap between the people and the police, which would be discussed further in this chapter.

4.5 If Reported, Police Approach Towards Reporting of Incident

In Part 1 of this segment, the respondents' experience with the police was studied. The approach of the police toward the *Northeast people* reporting the incident of hate crime was analyzed, and in Part 2 of this segment, police approach toward the *general population* is discussed when they encountered or witnessed hate crimes against Northeasterners. A total of 900 respondents were taken for the purpose of this data analyzation. In the data, there were such respondents who did not feel comfortable answering the question and were symbolized by the value 0 (Box 4.2).

Box 4.2: Types of Police Responses Studied

1. Police personnel refused to file a complaint or FIR.
2. Police demanded money to do their duties.
3. Police did not consider people suffering from hate crimes as actual victims.
4. Police did not consider hate crime or racial abuse as a crime.
5. Police blamed Northeast Indian victim for being a Northeasterner for this incident to had occurred.
6. Police did not pay heed to the victims because of their language or accent.
7. Police personnel took appropriate action.

According to Northeast people in Bangalore, 6% of the police personnel refused to file a complaint or FIR, 0.7% demanded money to do their duties, 0.7% did not consider people suffering from hate crime as actual victims, 0.7% did not consider hate crime or racial abuse as a crime, 0.7% blamed the Northeast people for being from the Northeastern states for such an incident to have occurred, 0% did not pay heed to the victims because of their language or accent, and 0% of the police personnel took appropriate action.

According to the Northeast people in Chennai, 2% of the police personnel refused to file a complaint or FIR, 0.7% demanded money to do their duties, 0.7% did not consider people suffering from hate crime as actual victims, 0% did not consider hate crime or racial abuse as a crime, 1.3% blamed the Northeast people for being from the Northeastern states for such an incident to had occurred, 0% did not pay heed to the victims because of their language or accent, and 0.7% of the police personnel took appropriate action.

According to the Northeast people in Delhi, 4% of the police personnel refused to file a complaint or FIR, 0% demanded money to do their duties, 0% did not consider people suffering from hate crime as actual victims, 0% did not consider hate crime or racial abuse as a crime, 0% blamed the Northeast people for being from the Northeastern states for such an incident to have occurred, 0% did not pay heed to the victims because of their language or accent, and 0% of the police personnel took appropriate action.

According to the Northeast people in Hyderabad, 0.7% of the police personnel refused to file a complaint or FIR, 0% demanded money to do their duties, 0% did not consider people suffering from hate crime as actual victims, 0% did not consider hate crime or racial abuse as a crime, 0% blamed the Northeast people for being from the Northeastern states for such an incident to have occurred, 0% did not pay heed to the victims because of their language or accent, and 1.3% of the police personnel took appropriate action.

According to the Northeast people in Mumbai, 0.7% of the police personnel refused to file a complaint or FIR, 0% demanded money to do their duties, 2% did not consider people suffering from hate crime as actual victims, 1.3% did not consider hate crime or racial abuse as a crime, 0.7% blamed the Northeast people for being from the Northeastern states for such an incident to have occurred, 0.7% did not pay heed to the victims because of their language or accent, and 2% of the police personnel took appropriate action.

According to the Northeast people in Pune, 4% of the police personnel refused to file a complaint or FIR, 0% demanded money to do their duties, 1.3% did not consider people suffering from hate crime as actual victims, 0% did not consider hate crime or racial abuse as a crime, 0% blamed the Northeast people for being from the Northeastern states for such an incident to have occurred, 0.7% did not pay heed to the victims because of their language or accent, and 0.7% of the police personnel took appropriate action.

4.5.1 Interpretation

From the above data, it could be observed that approach of the police toward victims of hate crime incidents was extremely discouraging. The fact that the Northeast people receive such reactions from the police was the reason that redressal in such scenarios becomes impossible. This was why in the previous segment, the Northeast people chose not to report the incident to the police. No matter how much the concerned authorities bring in innovative substantive laws, the remedies and protection would not reach the concerned section of the society till the time procedural drawbacks were improved. This requires extensive training of the stakeholders of the criminal justice system, i.e., the police, in handling such sensitive issue occurring in the society.

In Part 2 of this segment, the general population experience with the police was analyzed. The approach of police toward the general people reporting the incident of hate crime against the Northeast people was analyzed in the above tabular representation. The general people would be those persons who encountered such a crime committed against an acquaintance or those who witnessed the hate crime incident as a by-stander.

A total of 300 respondents were taken for the purpose of this data analyzation. In the data, there were such respondents who did not feel comfortable answering the question and were symbolized by the value 0.

According to the general people in Bangalore, 6% of the police personnel refused to file a complaint or FIR, 0.7% demanded money to do their duties, 0.7% did not consider people suffering from hate crime as actual victims, 0.7% did not consider hate crime or racial abuse as a crime, 0.7% blamed the Northeast people for being from the Northeastern states for such an incident to have occurred, and 2% of the police personnel took appropriate action.

According to the general people in Chennai, 2% of the police personnel refused to file a complaint or FIR, 0.7% demanded money to do their duties, 0.7% did not consider people suffering from hate crime as actual victims, 0% did not consider hate crime or racial abuse as a crime, 2% blamed the Northeast people for being from the Northeastern states for such an incident to have occurred, and 2% of the police personnel took appropriate action.

According to the general people in Delhi, 2% of the police personnel refused to file a complaint or FIR, 0% demanded money to do their duties, 2% did not consider people suffering from hate crime as actual victims, 4% did not consider hate crime or racial abuse as a crime, 0% blamed the Northeast people for being from the Northeastern states for such an incident to have occurred, and 2% of the police personnel took appropriate action.

According to the general people in Hyderabad, 4% of the police personnel refused to file a complaint or FIR, 2% demanded money to do their duties, 0% did not consider people suffering from hate crime as actual victims, 2% did not consider hate crime or racial abuse as a crime, 2% blamed the Northeast people for being from the Northeastern states for such an incident to have occurred, and 6% of the police personnel took appropriate action.

According to the general people in Mumbai, 0% of the police personnel refused to file a complaint or FIR, 0% demanded money to do their duties, 0% did not consider people suffering from hate crime as actual victims, 0% did not consider hate crime or racial abuse as a crime, 0% blamed the Northeast people for being from the Northeastern states for such an incident to have occurred, and 0% of the police personnel took appropriate action.

According to the general people in Pune, 2% of the police personnel refused to file a complaint or FIR, 0% demanded money to do their duties, 0% did not consider people suffering from hate crime as actual victims, 0% did not consider hate crime or racial abuse as a crime, 0% blamed the Northeast people for being from the Northeastern states for such an incident to have occurred, and 0% of the police personnel took appropriate action.

4.5.2 *Interpretation*

From the above data, it could be observed that approach of the police toward any information regarding victims of hate crime incidents or commission of the incident was extremely discouraging. The fact that people receive such reactions from the police was the reason that redressal in such scenarios becomes impossible. No matter how much the concerned authorities bring in innovative substantive laws, the remedies and protection would not reach the concerned section of the society till the time procedural drawbacks were improved. This requires extensive training of the stakeholders of the criminal justice system, i.e., the police, in handling such sensitive issue occurring in the society.

4.6 When Approached to Complaint, Police Treatment

In the above Fig. 4.4, data had been gathered which indicate toward the police treatment that the Northeast Indian victims had to go through after approaching the police for the purpose of reporting the incident of hate crime.

A total of 900 respondents were taken for the purpose of this data analyzation. In the data, there were such respondents who did not feel comfortable answering the question and were symbolized by the value 0.

In Bangalore, 2% of the Northeast people experienced misbehavior by the police, and 3.4% experienced the police being insensitive toward them and the issue of hate crime; however, 6% of the Northeast people responded that the police were understanding toward them. In Chennai, 4% of the Northeast people experienced misbehavior by the police, and 4% experienced the police being insensitive toward them and the issue of hate crime; however, 5.3% of the Northeast people responded that the police were understanding toward them.

In Delhi, 0% of the Northeast people experienced misbehavior by the police, and 1.3% experienced the police being insensitive toward them and the issue of hate crime; however, 6% of the Northeast people responded that the police were understanding toward them.

In Hyderabad, 2% of the Northeast people experienced misbehavior with by the police, and 0.7% experienced the police being insensitive toward them and the issue of hate crime; however, 0.7% of the Northeast people responded that the police were understanding toward them.

In Mumbai, 4% of the Northeast people experienced misbehavior by the police, 3.3% experienced the police being insensitive toward them and the issue of hate

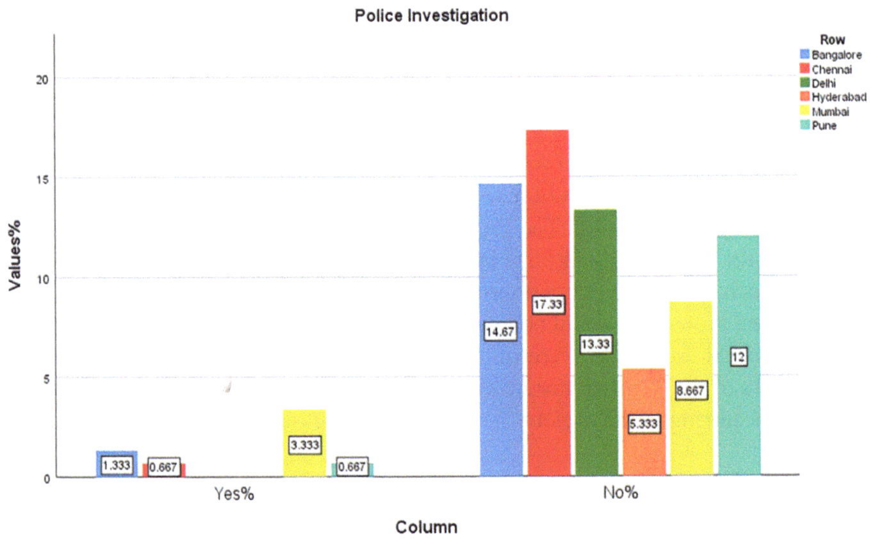

Fig. 4.4 Police treatment towards the Northeast Indian victim of hate crime

crime, and 0% of the Northeast people responded that the police were understanding toward them.

In Pune, 3.3% of the Northeast people experienced misbehavior by the police, and 2% experienced the police being insensitive toward them and the issue of hate crime; however, 6.7% of the Northeast people responded that the police were understanding toward them. The same data was represented graphically in Fig. 4.6.

4.6.1 Interpretation

This data was indicative toward the secondary victimization that the Northeast Indians had to go through in the process of grief redressal mechanism of the criminal justice system. After analyzing the data, it could be observed that the police were most understanding in Pune and least understanding and sensitive toward the hate crime victims in Mumbai. Unfortunately, such situation exists that there was a large population of the Northeast Indian victims of hate crimes who suffer from misbehavior and insensitivity at the hands of the police. Such a treatment instilled a feeling of insecurity among the victims of such a crime.

4.7 If Reported, Then Status of Investigation (Fig. 4.5)

In the above Table 4.3, data had been collected so as to indicate if police conducted an investigation for the complaint against hate crime incident reported by the *Northeast people*. A total of 900 respondents were taken for the purpose of this data

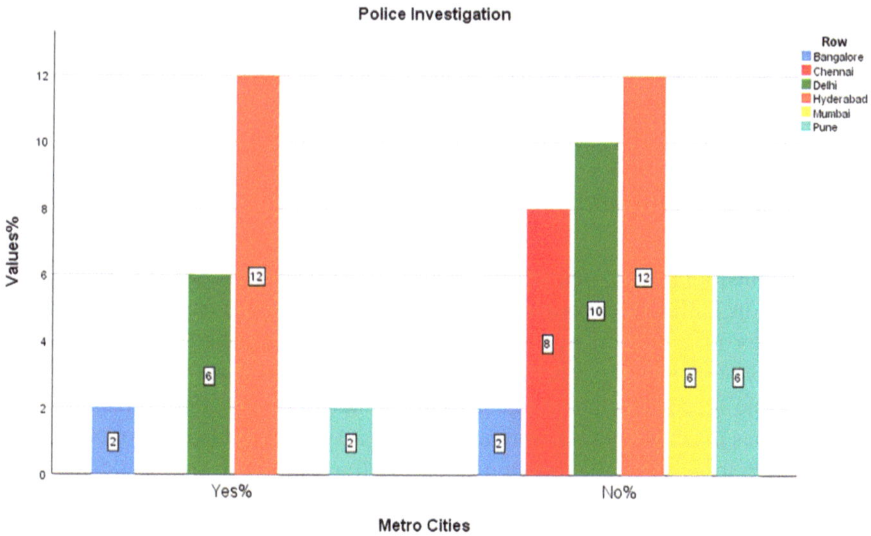

Fig. 4.5 Police investigation after complaint by the Northeast people

Table 4.3 Whether investigation was conducted by the police after reporting of hate crime incident by *Northeast people*

	0		Yes		No		Total	
Police investigation	N	Percentage	N	Percentage	N	Percentage	N	Percentage
Bangalore	126	84.0	2	1.3	22	14.7	150	100.0
Chennai	123	82.0	1	0.7	26	17.3	150	100.0
Delhi	130	86.7	0	0.0	20	13.3	150	100.0
Hyderabad	142	94.7	0	0.0	8	5.3	150	100.0
Mumbai	132	88.0	5	3.3	13	8.7	150	100.0
Pune	131	87.3	1	0.7	18	12.0	150	100.0

analyzation. In the data, there were such respondents who did not feel comfortable answering the question and were symbolized by the value 0.

In Bangalore, 1.3% of the Northeast people responded that investigation was done by the police, whereas 14.7% of the Northeast people responded that investigation was not done by the police regarding the incident of hate crime.

In Chennai, 0.7% of the Northeast people responded that investigation was done by the police, whereas 17.3% of the Northeast people responded that investigation was not done by the police regarding the incident of hate crime.

In Delhi, 0% of the Northeast people responded that investigation was done by the police, whereas 13.3% of the Northeast people responded that investigation was not done by the police regarding the incident of hate crime.

In Hyderabad, 0% of the Northeast people responded that investigation was done by the police, whereas 5.3% of the Northeast people responded that investigation was not done by the police regarding the incident of hate crime.

In Mumbai, 3.3% of the Northeast people responded that investigation was done by the police, whereas 8.7% of the Northeast people responded that investigation was not done by the police regarding the incident of hate crime.

In Pune, 0.7% of the Northeast people responded that investigation was done by the police, whereas 12% of the Northeast people responded that investigation was not done by the police regarding the incident of hate crime.

4.7.1 Interpretation

The aforementioned data denotes the inconsistency in the criminal procedural law that exists in India. Most people responded that their complaints or FIR were not furthered by investigation by the police. A very small number of people got the opportunity of their matter reaching the investigation stage. Pune was the city where most people responded that investigation was conducted by the Police, whereas Chennai was the city where investigation was least conducted by the police according to the respondents. This highlights the condition in which such incidents were handled by the police. It was a blatant misuse of the power that was given to the

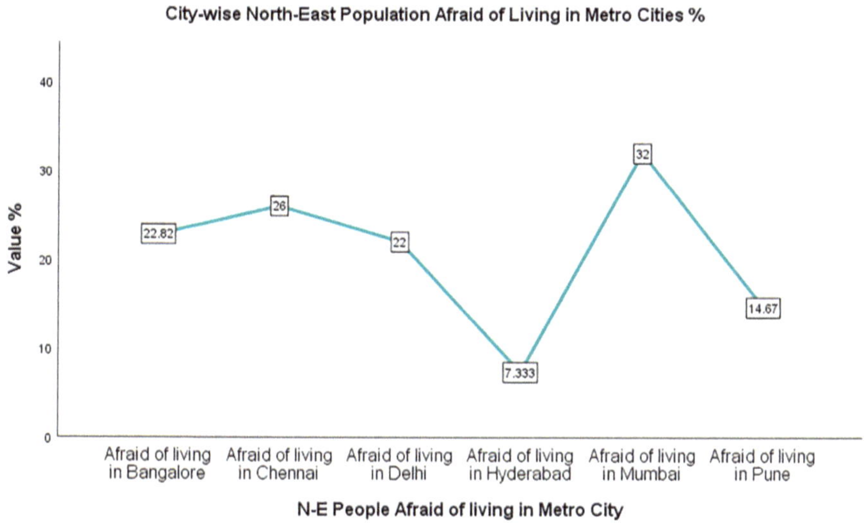

Fig. 4.6 Police investigation on complaint by the general people

Table 4.4 Whether investigation was conducted by the police after reporting of hate crime incident against the Northeast people by the *general population*

	0		Yes		No		Total	
Police investigation	N	Percentage	N	Percentage	N	Percentage	N	Percentage
Bangalore	48	96.0	1	2.0	1	2.0	50	100.0
Chennai	46	92.0	0	0.0	4	8.0	50	100.0
Delhi	42	84.0	3	6.0	5	10.0	50	100.0
Hyderabad	38	76.0	6	12.0	6	12.0	50	100.0
Mumbai	47	94.0	0	0.0	3	6.0	50	100.0
Pune	46	92.0	1	2.0	3	6.0	50	100.0

police for the purpose of providing adequate protection and remedies to the Northeast Indians in metro cities (Fig. 4.6).

Table 4.4 shows the data in the case where general people after having witnessed the hate crime incident against a Northeast Indian or encountered it with a close acquaintance. Complainants were the *general population* people in this section. A total of 300 respondents were taken for the purpose of this data analyzation. In the data, there were such respondents who did not feel comfortable answering the question and were symbolized by the value 0.

In Bangalore, 2% of the general people responded that investigation was done by the police, whereas another 2% of the general people responded that investigation was not done by the police regarding the incident of hate crime.

In Chennai, 0% of the general people responded that investigation was done by the police, whereas 8% of the general people responded that investigation was not done by the police regarding the incident of hate crime.

In Delhi, 6% of the general people responded that investigation was done by the police, whereas 10% of the general people responded that investigation was not done by the police regarding the incident of hate crime.

In Hyderabad, 12% of the general people responded that investigation was done by the police, whereas another 12% of the general people responded that investigation was not done by the police regarding the incident of hate crime.

In Mumbai, 0% of the general people responded that investigation was done by the police, whereas 6% of the general people responded that investigation was not done by the police regarding the incident of hate crime.

In Pune, 2% of the general people responded that investigation was done by the police, whereas 6% of the general people responded that investigation was not done by the police regarding the incident of hate crime.

4.7.2 Interpretation

The aforementioned data denotes the inconsistency in the criminal procedural law that exists in India. Most people responded that the complaints or FIR were not furthered by investigation by the police. A very small number of people saw the matter reaching the investigation stage. Hyderabad was the city where most people responded that investigation was conducted by the police, whereas Delhi was the city where investigation was conducted lesser in proportion by the police according to the respondents. This highlights the condition in which such incidents were handled by the police. It was a blatant misuse of the power that was given to the police for the purpose of providing adequate protection and remedies to the Northeast Indians in metro cities.

4.8 Investigation Result

In this segment, data was interpreted in order to gather an account of how much time did the police take to conduct the investigation as well as to examine the result of the investigation with respect to hate crime incidents against the Northeast people. *Northeastern Indians* were the complainants in this case. A total of 900 respondents were taken for the purpose of this data analyzation. In the data, there were such respondents who did not feel comfortable answering the question and were symbolized by the value 0.

In Bangalore, 0.7% of the Northeast people received positive result from the investigation in 24 h; 0% got positive results in 1 month; 0.7% got positive result in 1 year; and 2% received negative result from the investigation.

In Chennai, none of the respondents answered the question.

In Delhi, 0% of the Northeast people received positive result from the investigation in 24 h; 0% got positive results in 1 month; 0% got positive result in 1 year; and 2% received negative result from the investigation.

In Hyderabad, 0% of the Northeast people received positive result from the investigation in 24 h; 0% got positive results in 1 month; 0% got positive result in 1 year; and 0.7% received negative result from the investigation.

In Mumbai, 1.3% of the Northeast people received positive result from the investigation in 24 h; 0% got positive results in 1 month; 0.7% got positive result in 1 year; and 2% received negative result from the investigation.

In Pune, 0% of the Northeast people received positive result from the investigation in 24 h; 0% got positive results in 1 month; 0% got positive result in 1 year; and 0.7% received negative result from the investigation.

4.8.1 Interpretation

It could be observed after analyzing the data that most of the people got positive result from the investigation. The investigation process might consume time which could range up to one year. However, there was also fair percentage of the investigation entailing negative result in the six metro cities. This means that although there were some steps being taken toward a fair and just criminal procedural system, there still remain certain areas where the mechanism was lacking. Such areas must be tackled along with substantive safety measures.

In another part of this segment, data had been collected by researchers in order to examine the result of the investigation with respect to hate crime incidents against the Northeast people. This investigation was related to the complaints made by the *general population* who had either encountered or witnessed hate crime incidents against the Northeast people. A total of 300 respondents were taken for the purpose of this data analyzation. In the data, there were such respondents who did not feel comfortable answering the question and were symbolized by the value 0.

In Bangalore, 2% of the general people received positive result, whereas 0% of the general people received negative result. In Chennai, 0% of the general people received positive result, whereas 6% of the general people received negative result. In Delhi, 4% of the general people received positive result, whereas 0% of the general people received negative result. In Hyderabad, 4% of the general people received positive result, whereas 6% of the general people received negative result. In Mumbai, none of the general people respond to the question. In Pune, 2% of the general people received positive result, whereas 0% of the general people received negative result.

4.8.2 *Interpretation*

From the above data, it could be understood that there was a mixed response on the question of result of investigation by the police with respect to hate crime incidents against the Northeast people.

Delhi was the city where fairly more percentage of general people had responded positively to the investigation result as compared to other cities. Hyderabad and Chennai were the cities where negative responses had been received with regard to investigation result.

It becomes evident that the inconsistency in the investigation result could be due to a number of reasons related to nature of the cases. But other than that, improvement in the investigation mechanism would create a big difference in the outcome of such cases.

4.9 If Not Reported to Police, Why?

In this segment, reasons for both the Northeasterners and the general population have been discussed. These reasons indicate why the victims, first responders, or the spectators hesitated the enforcement mechanism that is in place for the redressal of such complaints. These will enunciate where our legal machinery is lacking in protection against hate crime incidents against the Northeast Indians in metropolitan cities.

4.9.1 *Northeast People Did Not Report the Incident*

In Table 4.5, reasons for the Northeast people to not report the incident to the police were discussed. A total of 900 respondents were taken for the purpose of this data analyzation. In the data, there were such respondents who did not feel comfortable answering the question – which were symbolized by the value 0.

In Bangalore, 13.3% of the Northeast people were fearful or uncomfortable reporting the incident to the police, 12% of the people believe that the police was not serious about their problems, 6.7% felt that reporting to the police was a difficult process, 15.3% responded that they had accepted the hate crimes that were committed against them and resorted to ignore the issue instead of reporting to the police, and 2.7% approached other local agencies rather than the police.

In Chennai, 8.7% of the Northeast people were fearful or uncomfortable reporting the incident to the police, 14% of the people believe that the police was not serious about their problems, 3.3% felt that reporting to the police was a difficult process, 13.3% responded that they had accepted the hate crimes that were

Table 4.5 Reason the Northeast people did not report the incident to the police

Why incidents not reported to the police		N	Percentage
Bangalore	0	75	50.0
	Fearful or uncomfortable	20	13.3
	Police not serious	18	12.0
	Difficult process	10	6.7
	Accepted and ignored	23	15.3
	Approached local agencies	4	2.7
Chennai	0	90	60.0
	Fearful or uncomfortable	13	8.7
	Police not serious	21	14.0
	Difficult process	5	3.3
	Accepted and ignored	20	13.3
	Approached local agencies	1	0.7
Delhi	0	78	52.3
	Fearful or uncomfortable	22	14.8
	Police not serious	30	20.1
	Difficult process	1	0.7
	Accepted and ignored	18	12.1
	Approached local agencies	0	0.0
Hyderabad	0	104	69.3
	Fearful or uncomfortable	11	7.3
	Police not serious	11	7.3
	Difficult process	4	2.7
	Accepted and ignored	19	12.7
	Approached local agencies	1	0.7
Mumbai	0	84	56.0
	Fearful or uncomfortable	9	6.0
	Police not serious	39	26.0
	Difficult process	9	6.0
	Accepted and ignored	9	6.0
	Approached local agencies	0	0.0
Pune	0	101	67.3
	Fearful or uncomfortable	5	3.3
	Police not serious	21	14.0
	Difficult process	4	2.7
	Accepted and ignored	18	12.0
	Approached local agencies	1	0.7
	Total	900	100.0

committed against them and resorted to ignore the issue instead of reporting to the police, and 0.7% approached other local agencies rather than the police.

In Delhi, 14.8% of the Northeast people were fearful or uncomfortable reporting the incident to the police, 20.1% of the people believe that the police was not serious about their problems, 0.7% felt that reporting to the police was a difficult process, 12.1% responded that they had accepted the hate crimes that were committed against them and resorted to ignore the issue instead of reporting to the police, and 0% approached other local agencies rather than the police.

In Hyderabad, 7.3% of the Northeast people were fearful or uncomfortable reporting the incident to the police, 7.3% of the people believe that the police was not serious about their problems, 2.7% felt that reporting to the police was a difficult process, 12.7% responded that they had accepted the hate crimes that were committed against them and resorted to ignore the issue instead of reporting to the police, and 0.7% approached other local agencies rather than the police.

In Mumbai, 6% of the Northeast people were fearful or uncomfortable reporting the incident to the police, 26% of the people believe that the police was not serious about their problems, 6% felt that reporting to the police was a difficult process, 6% responded that they had accepted the hate crimes that were committed against them and resorted to ignore the issue instead of reporting to the police, and 0% approached other local agencies rather than the police.

In Pune, 3.3% of the Northeast people were fearful or uncomfortable reporting the incident to the police, 14% people believe that the police was not serious about their problems, 2.7% felt that reporting to the police was a difficult process, 12% responded that they had accepted the hate crimes that were committed against them and resorted to ignore the issue instead of reporting to the police, and 0.7% approached other local agencies rather than the police.

4.9.1.1 Interpretation

From the above data researchers had analyzed that most Northeast people in Delhi did not report the hate crime incident to the police because of the reason that they were either fearful of the police or were uncomfortable to report the incident. Most Northeast people in Mumbai did not report the hate crime incident to the police because of the reason that police were not serious.

Most Northeast people in Bangalore did not report the hate crime incident to the police because of the reason that the process was difficult. Most Northeast people in Bangalore also did not report the hate crime incident to the police because of the reason that they had accepted the problem of discrimination against the Northeastern people in metro cities and chose to ignore these hate crime incidents. Most Northeast people in Bangalore did not report the hate crime incident to the police because of the reason that they approached other local agencies.

Different problems related to the Northeast people not reporting the incident to police was distributed among the six metro cities. Focus should be not only to improve the system but also to encourage the Northeast people to come forward and seek appropriate redressal.

4.9.2 General Population Did Not Report the Incident

The same study was conducted for the general people to find out the reasons to not report the incident to the police. A total of 300 respondents were taken for the purpose of this data analyzation. In the data, there were such respondents who did not feel comfortable answering the question and were symbolized by the value 0. The *general people* were analyzed on the hate crime incidents they witnessed or encountered against the Northeast people.

In Bangalore, 2% of the general people were fearful or uncomfortable reporting the incident to the police, 2% of the people believe that the police was not serious of their problems, 0% felt that reporting to the police was a difficult process, 4% responded that they had accepted the hate crimes that were committed against the Northeast population and chose to ignore the issue instead of reporting to the police, and 4% approached other local agencies rather than the police.

In Chennai, 6% of the general people were fearful or uncomfortable reporting the incident to the police, 6% of the people believe that the police was not serious of their problems, 4% felt that reporting to the police was a difficult process, 2% responded that they had accepted the hate crimes that were committed against them and chose to ignore the issue instead of reporting to the police, and 2% approached other local agencies rather than the police.

In Delhi, 22% of the general people were fearful or uncomfortable reporting the incident to the police, 10% of the people believe that the police was not serious of their problems, 0% felt that reporting to the police was a difficult process, 14% responded that they had accepted the hate crimes that were committed against them and chose to ignore the issue instead of reporting to the police, and 10% approached other local agencies rather than the police.

In Hyderabad, 10% of the general people were fearful or uncomfortable reporting the incident to the police, 4% of the people believe that the police was not serious of their problems, 4% felt that reporting to the police was a difficult process, 4% responded that they had accepted the hate crimes that were committed against them and chose to ignore the issue instead of reporting to the police, and 2% approached other local agencies rather than the police.

In Mumbai, 2% of the general people were fearful or uncomfortable reporting the incident to the police, 2% of the people believe that the police was not serious of their problems, 2% felt that reporting to the police was a difficult process, 0% responded that they had accepted the hate crimes that were committed against them and chose to ignore the issue instead of reporting to the police, and 4% approached other local agencies rather than the police.

In Pune, 0% of the general people were fearful or uncomfortable reporting the incident to the police, 6% of the people believe that the police was not serious of their problems, 2% felt that reporting to the police was a difficult process, 0% responded that they had accepted the hate crimes that were committed against them and chose to ignore the issue instead of reporting to the police, and 0% approached other local agencies rather than the police.

4.9.2.1 Interpretation

From the above, it was analyzed that most general people in Delhi did not report the hate crime incident to the police because of the reason that they were either fearful of the police or were uncomfortable to report the incident.

Most general people in Delhi did not report the hate crime incident to the police because of the police were not serious. Most general people in Delhi also did not report the hate crime incident to the police because of the reason that they had accepted the problem of discrimination against the Northeastern people in metro cities and chose to ignore these hate crime incidents.

Most general people in Chennai and Hyderabad did not report the hate crime incident to the police because of the reason that the process was difficult.

Most general people in Delhi also did not report the hate crime incident to the police because of the reason that they approached other local agencies. It could be seen that most general people from Delhi did not report the crime to the police because of numerous reasons. These reasons should be taken into consideration while spreading awareness about the problem of hate crime against the Northeast Indian people in metro cities.

4.10 Victimization

In this segment, it shows three aspects to signify how the Northeastern population in Indian metropolitan cities are victimized – their fear of living in the six metropolitan cities, how often this fear grips them while residing in these cities, and how afraid they are on a daily basis to be subjected to hate crime violence because of their identity. This topic is taken extensively from every angle possible in order to deeply understand the metal anguish of the Northeasterners in India.

4.10.1 Fear of Living in Metropolitan Cities

The data collected clearly showed the percentage of the Northeast people living in metropolitan cities afraid of living in these cities. A total of 900 respondents were taken for the purpose of this data analyzation. In the data, there were such respondents who did not feel comfortable answering the question and were symbolized by the value 0.

Of the total respondents, 26% of the Northeast people in Chennai were afraid of living in the city; 22.8% of the Northeast people in Bangalore were afraid of living in the city; 22% of the Northeast people in Delhi were afraid of living in the city; 7.3% of the Northeast people in Hyderabad were afraid of living in the city; 32% of the Northeast people in Mumbai were afraid of living in the city; and 14.7% of the

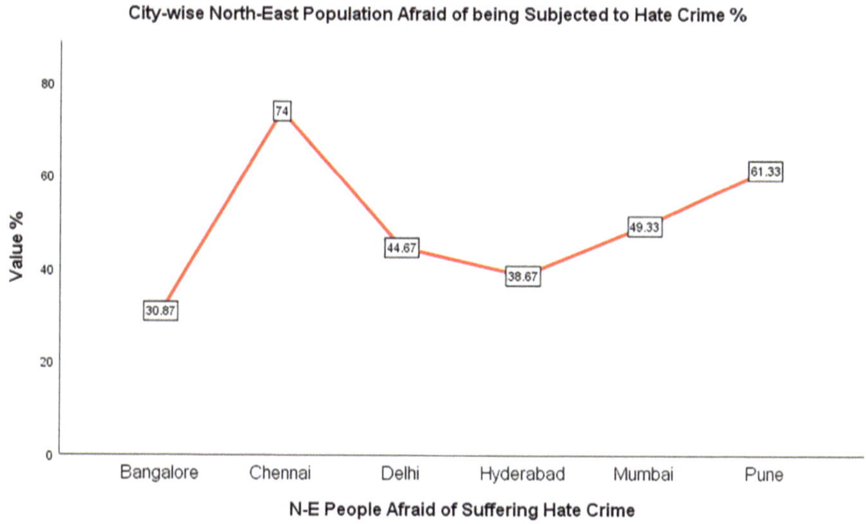

Fig. 4.7 Northeast people afraid of living in metro city

Northeast people in Pune were afraid of living in the city. Figure 4.7 was the graphical representation of the same.

4.10.1.1 Interpretation

After computing and analyzing the data above, it could be said that these hate crime and exploitative incidents against the Northeast Indian people had led to people feeling unsafe in the city they live in. Most Northeastern people living in Mumbai feel unsafe and afraid. This was not a healthy indicator of a secular and lawful society. These were some of the ways that secondary victimization takes place where the person who was affected by the incident were further affected and the consequences of which could be seen in other areas of life. Such insecurity spreads among the people that were around the victims as well.

4.10.2 How Often Were the Northeast People Worried About Staying in Metropolitan Cities

In this study, data with respect to how frequently people had been worried about living in their city was analyzed. A total of 900 respondents were taken for the purpose of this data analyzation. In the data, there were such respondents who did not feel comfortable answering the question and were symbolized by the value 0.

In Bangalore, 3.4% of the Northeast people worry very often living in their city, 20.1% worry often staying in their city, 8.7% worry rarely residing in their city, and 1.3% worry very rarely staying in their city.

In Chennai, 4.7% of the Northeast people worry very often living in their city, 34% worry often staying in their city, 25.3% worry rarely residing in their city, and 14% worry very rarely staying in their city.

In Delhi, 6.7% of the Northeast people worry very often living in their city, 25.3% worry often staying in their city, 10.7% worry rarely residing in their city, and 5.3% worry very rarely staying in their city.

In Hyderabad, 15.3% of the Northeast people worry very often living in their city, 28% worry often staying in their city, 7.3% worry rarely residing in their city, and 4.7% worry very rarely staying in their city.

In Mumbai, 7.3% of the Northeast people worry very often living in their city, 15.3% worry often staying in their city, 18% worry rarely residing in their city, and 13.3% worry very rarely staying in their city.

In Pune, 9.3% of the Northeast people worry very often living in their city, 29.3% worry often staying in their city, 18% worry rarely residing in their city, and 11.3% worry very rarely staying in their city.

4.10.2.1 Interpretation

After careful analyzation and computation of the data given above, it could be understood that most people from Hyderabad worry very often living in the metro city; most people from Chennai worry often living in the metro city; most people from Chennai worry rarely living in the metro city; and most people from Pune worry very rarely living in the metro city.

This was indicative toward the scenario where frequency percentage of the people afraid of living in the metro city was examined so as to understand how bad the situation is. The data denotes the worse situation that could arise for any citizen of the country. Such a result points toward the urgency of the matter.

4.10.3 Afraid of Being Subjected to Hate Crime Because of Identity

Upon assessing the data, it examined whether the Northeast people feel afraid of being subjected to hate crime because of their identity. A total of 900 respondents were taken for the purpose of this data analyzation. In the data, there were such respondents who did not feel comfortable answering the question and were symbolized by the value 0.

Of the total respondents interviewed, 30.9% of the Northeast people in Bangalore were afraid of being subjected to hate crime because of their identity; 74% of the

		Metro City													
		Pune		Mumbai		New Delhi		Bangalore		Chennai		Hyderabad		Total	
After Effects of the Incident		Count	Table N %	Count	Table N %	Count	Table N %	Count	Table N %	Count	Table N %	Count	Table N %	Count	Table N %
Avoided going out at night	0	49	5.4%	49	5.4%	50	5.6%	33	3.7%	6	0.7%	74	8.2%	261	29.0%
	Yes	36	4.0%	41	4.6%	38	4.2%	19	2.1%	37	4.1%	21	2.3%	192	21.3%
	No	65	7.2%	60	6.7%	62	6.9%	98	10.9%	107	11.9%	55	6.1%	447	49.7%
You Avoid going to place/s where you experienced the hate crime	0	49	5.4%	48	5.3%	50	5.6%	32	3.6%	6	0.7%	74	8.2%	259	28.8%
	Yes	28	3.1%	40	4.4%	19	2.1%	31	3.4%	52	5.8%	17	1.9%	187	20.8%
	No	73	8.1%	62	6.9%	81	9.0%	87	9.7%	92	10.2%	59	6.6%	454	50.4%
Started going out at certain time of the day, which you to be considered safe	0	49	5.4%	48	5.3%	50	5.6%	32	3.6%	6	0.7%	74	8.2%	259	28.8%
	Yes	16	1.8%	22	2.4%	14	1.6%	12	1.3%	35	3.9%	9	1.0%	108	12.0%
	No	85	9.4%	80	8.9%	86	9.6%	106	11.8%	109	12.1%	67	7.4%	533	59.2%
Changed your schedule	0	49	5.4%	48	5.3%	50	5.6%	32	3.6%	6	0.7%	74	8.2%	259	28.8%
	Yes	8	0.9%	16	1.8%	5	0.6%	11	1.2%	41	4.6%	6	0.7%	87	9.7%
	No	93	10.3%	86	9.6%	95	10.6%	107	11.9%	103	11.4%	70	7.8%	554	61.6%
Stopped going out alone	0	49	5.4%	49	5.4%	50	5.6%	32	3.6%	6	0.7%	74	8.2%	260	28.9%
	Yes	26	2.9%	28	3.1%	16	1.8%	27	3.0%	46	5.1%	15	1.7%	158	17.6%
	No	75	8.3%	73	8.1%	84	9.3%	91	10.1%	98	10.9%	61	6.8%	482	53.6%
Retaliated against it	0	49	5.4%	49	5.4%	50	5.6%	32	3.6%	6	0.7%	74	8.2%	260	28.9%
	Yes	7	0.8%	7	0.8%	11	1.2%	11	1.2%	2	0.2%	10	1.1%	48	5.3%
	No	94	10.4%	94	10.4%	89	9.9%	107	11.9%	142	15.8%	66	7.3%	592	65.8%
Avoided the situation	0	49	5.4%	47	5.2%	50	5.6%	32	3.6%	6	0.7%	74	8.2%	258	28.7%
	Yes	39	4.3%	52	5.8%	52	5.8%	37	4.1%	74	8.2%	36	4.0%	290	32.2%
	No	62	6.9%	51	5.7%	48	5.3%	81	9.0%	70	7.8%	40	4.4%	352	39.1%

Fig. 4.8 Afraid of being subjected to hate crime because of identity

Northeast people in Chennai were afraid of being subjected to hate crime because of their identity; 44.7% of the Northeast people in Delhi were afraid of being subjected to hate crime because of their identity; 38.7% of the Northeast people in Hyderabad were afraid of being subjected to hate crime because of their identity; 49.3% of the Northeast people in Mumbai were afraid of being subjected to hate crime because of their identity; and 61.3% of the Northeast people in Pune were afraid of being subjected to hate crime because of their identity. Figure 4.8 was the graphical representation of the same.

4.10.3.1 Interpretation

From the above data, it could be clearly seen that the Northeast people in Chennai were the most afraid of being subjected of hate crime because of their identity. This was a blow to the secularism and diversity of the Indian society. A section of people not feeling safe enough at the place of their residence because of their identity was indicative toward the urgency of the matter at hand. Citizenship given to people of India entails protection of their rights by the state, and this study was an example of where the state functionaries made for the people were going wrong. Keeping in mind this data, appropriate steps should be taken.

4.11 Hypothesis Testing

Advanced statistical analysis of $_{Hn02\ =}$ Dearth of legal protection had led to increase in hate crime incidents against the Northeast population. The hypothesis formulated was administered using correlation via SPSS software (Table 4.6) (Box 4.3).

Table 4.6 Correlation between adequacy of existing laws and hate crime incidents

Correlation			
		Adequacy of existing laws	Hate crime incidents
Adequacy of existing laws	Pearson correlation	1	.037
	Sig. (2-tailed)		.261
	N	900	900
Hate crime incidents	Pearson correlation	.037	1
	Sig. (2-tailed)	.261	
	N	900	900

Box 4.3: Statistical Result

1. Correlation of adequacy of existing laws with itself (r = 1) and the number of non-missing observations for adequacy of existing laws (n = 900).
2. Correlation of adequacy of existing and hate crime incidents (r = 0.037), based on n = 900 observations with pair-wise non-missing values.
3. Correlation of adequacy of existing and hate crime incidents (r = 0.037), based on n = 900 observations with pair-wise non-missing values.
4. Correlation of hate crime incidents with itself (r = 1) and the number of non-missing observations for hate crime incidents (n = 900).

Decision and Conclusion

Based on the results, we could state the following:

- Adequacies of existing laws and hate crime incidents had a statistically significant linear relationship ($p < .001$).
- The direction of the relationship was a weak positive correlation (i.e., adequacy of laws and hate crime incidents were positively correlated), meaning that these variables tend to increase together.
- The magnitude, or strength, of the association was approximately moderate ($.3 < | r | < .5$).

Chapter 5
Assessment of Legal Development and Services Provided Against Hate Crimes

5.1 Introduction

In this chapter, the research team had tried to bring forth the legal assistance provided to the victims of hate crime along with the services rendered. The chapter mentions various agencies that the Northeast people approached for reporting the incident and action taken by the agencies after reporting of the hate crime incidents across six metropolitan cities. The research team had also studied how much of a success the investigation process was after the reporting of the incidence was done.

The chapter further dealt with the awareness quotient of the Northeast people as well as the general population with regard to existing laws and the Bezbaruah Committee. It also analyzed whether there was a need for new laws specifically protecting the rights of the Northeast population. In this regard, the data of both the target groups had been taken into account, i.e., of the Northeast population and the general population residing in the six metropolitan cities.

5.2 Awareness of the Northeast Population About Existing Laws to Prevent Hate Crime

Figure 5.1 depicts the city-wise distribution of the Northeast Indian people who were aware of Section 153A of the Indian Penal Code, 1860, as a legal remedy that could be used to tackle the problem of hate crime against the Northeast population. A total of 900 respondents had been taken for the purpose of this data analyzation. In the data, there were some respondents who did not feel comfortable answering the question, and their responses were symbolized by the value 0. In Bangalore, 10.1% of the Northeast people were aware of the said law; 9.3% of the Northeast people were aware in Chennai, 25.3% were aware in Delhi, 13.3% in Hyderabad,

G. S. Bajpai et al., *Hate Crime in India*,
https://doi.org/10.1007/978-3-031-30522-1_5

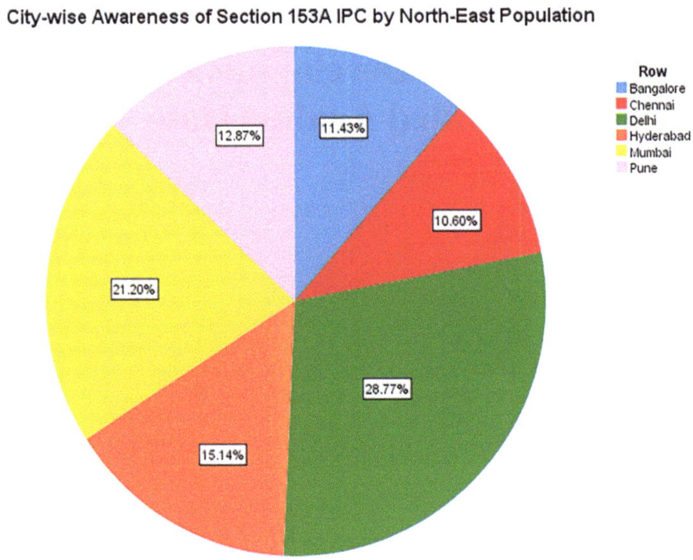

Fig. 5.1 Awareness about Section 153A IPC to prevent hate crime

18.7% in Mumbai, and 11.3% in Pune were aware of the law. This means to say that most Northeast people from Delhi were aware of the law. On the contrary, 82.6% of the Northeast Indians in Bangalore, 88.7% in Chennai, 67.3% in Delhi, 66.7% in Hyderabad, 58.7% in Mumbai, and 76% of the Northeast people in Pune were not aware of Section 153A IPC. It could be observed that Chennai had the least aware Northeast population in this regard.

Figure 5.2 depicts the city-wise distribution of the Northeast Indian people who were aware of the Scheduled Castes and Scheduled Tribes (Prevention of Atrocities) Act, 1989 as a legal remedy that could be used to tackle the problem of hate crime against the Northeast population. A total of 900 respondents were taken for the purpose of this data analyzation. In the data, there were such respondents who did not feel comfortable answering the question and their responses were symbolized by the value 0. In Bangalore, 23.5% of the Northeast people were aware about the said act; 42% of the Northeast people were aware in Chennai, 44.7% were aware in Delhi, 26% in Hyderabad, 23.3% in Mumbai, and 20.7% in Pune were aware of the act. This means to say that most Northeast people from Delhi were aware of the law. On the contrary, 68.5% of the Northeast Indians in Bangalore were not aware of this act; 56% in Chennai, 47.3% in Delhi, 53.3% in Hyderabad, 54% in Mumbai, and 66% of the Northeast people in Pune were not aware of the Scheduled Castes and Scheduled Tribes (Prevention of Atrocities) Act, 1989. It could be observed that Delhi had the most aware Northeast population in this regard.

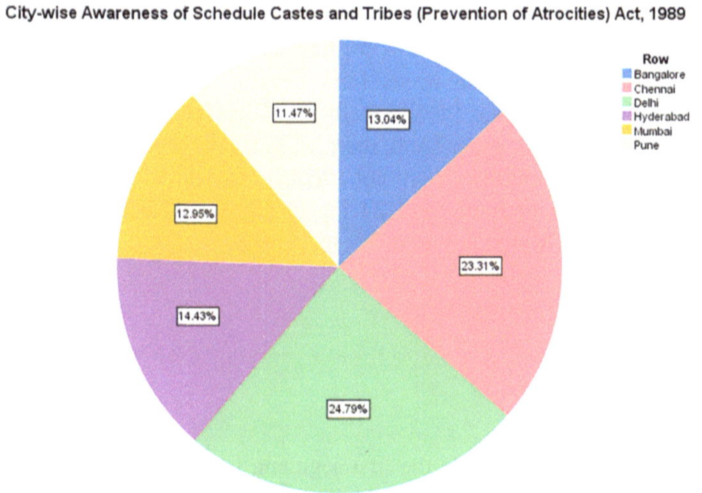

Fig. 5.2 Awareness about Scheduled Castes and Scheduled Tribes (Prevention of Atrocities) Act, 1989 to prevent hate crime

5.2.1 Interpretation

In the aforementioned segment, the researchers had aimed to study to what extent the Northeast people in metropolitan cities were aware of the legal remedies that could safeguard them against the hate crimes. It was unfortunate to see that people had neither much knowledge of the criminal law provision, i.e., 153A IPC nor the special legislation for the protection of the specific class of people, i.e., Scheduled Caste and Scheduled Tribe Act. These acts were some of the ways by which the Northeast population could seek redressal in the event of an incident, there being lack of any other legal measure as a countermeasure of hate crimes against the Northeast people in India. Lack of awareness indicates how ineffectively the legal remedies were reaching the real victims of the crime. Awareness remains a very important aspect that ought to be dealt by the concerned authorities.

5.3 Adequacy of Existing Laws as per the Northeast Population

This chapter focused upon the efficiency of the legal infrastructures provided as a defense against hate crimes in India. A total of 900 respondents were taken for the purpose of this data analyzation. In the data, there were some respondents who did not feel comfortable answering the question and were symbolized by the value 0. It was seen that the Northeast people who believe that existing laws were appropriate in tackling hate crimes were 6.7% in Bangalore, 9.3% in Chennai, 24.7% in Delhi,

8% in Hyderabad, 18.7% in Mumbai, and 7.4% in Pune. There were also certain percentage of the Northeast people according to whom the laws were adequate in text but their implementation needs improvement. Such people were 4.7% in Bangalore, 5.3% in Chennai, 14% in Delhi, 14% in Hyderabad, 3.3% in Mumbai, and 8.1% in Pune. On the other hand, there were 10.1% of the people in Bangalore who believes that current laws were not adequate to deal with hate crimes against the Northeast people in India, and 24.7% in Chennai, 5.3% in Delhi, 8.7% in Hyderabad, 5.3% in Mumbai, and 4.7% in Pune do not believe that current laws were adequate.

5.3.1 Interpretation

The laws that were discussed in the first segment, i.e., Section 153A of the Indian Penal Code, 1860 and the Scheduled Castes and Scheduled Tribes (Prevention of Atrocities) Act, 1989, were the existing legal remedies that was in question above. Northeast people were vulnerable since many incidents had surfaced over time. This means that it becomes imperative to understand if these laws provide some respite from the hate crime incidents. In order to gather data on these lines, perceptions of the Northeast people were taken into account in order to evaluate if the existing laws were adequate. It could be inferred that the Northeast people in Delhi were most inclined toward the view that current laws were adequate. Delhi and Hyderabad were the two metro cities which mostly believed that current laws were efficient only with improvement in its implementation. The Northeast people in Chennai mostly believe that current laws were not adequate, whereas Pune had the least number of people believing that current laws were not adequate. It could be clearly seen that there was lack of consensus or proper majority in one kind of perception. These responses were based on the individual experiences of the Northeasterners.

5.4 Adequacy of Existing Laws as per the General Population

Similar to the preceding segment, a total of 900 respondents were taken for the purpose of this section's data analyzation as well. In the data, there were such respondents who did not feel comfortable answering the question – which were symbolized by the value 0. In the study, it was seen that the general people who believe that existing laws were appropriate in tackling hate crimes were 42% in Bangalore, 28% in Chennai, 78% in Delhi, 70% in Hyderabad, 62% in Mumbai, and 46% in Pune. On the contrary, there were 44% of the general people in Bangalore who believe that current laws were not adequate to deal with hate crimes against the Northeast people in India, and 68% in Chennai, 20% in Delhi, 28% in Hyderabad, 24% in Mumbai, and 12% in Pune do not believe that current laws were adequate.

5.4.1 Interpretation

The general population in metro cities were asked the same question as the Northeast people in the context that the general people had either witnessed a Northeast acquaintance who had suffered from hate crime or had encountered hate crime being committed against the Northeast Indian as a by-stander. From the above data, it was clear that higher percentage of people in Delhi consider that the existing laws were adequate, whereas general people in Chennai were more inclined toward the perception that the existing laws were inadequate. In the scenario where they were put similar question as the Northeast Indians, a stark difference could be seen in the responses. Mostly general people had responded that the existing laws were adequate in preventing the hate crime incidents. This view was different from the mixed response received from the Northeast people in these metro cities. It showed how varied the points of view were among the Northeast and general people.

5.5 Awareness of the Northeast People Regarding the Bezbaruah Committee Recommendations

Figure 5.3 depicts the city-wise distribution of the Northeast Indian people who were aware of the Bezbaruah Committee Recommendations that could be used to tackle the problem of hate crime against the Northeast population. A total of 900

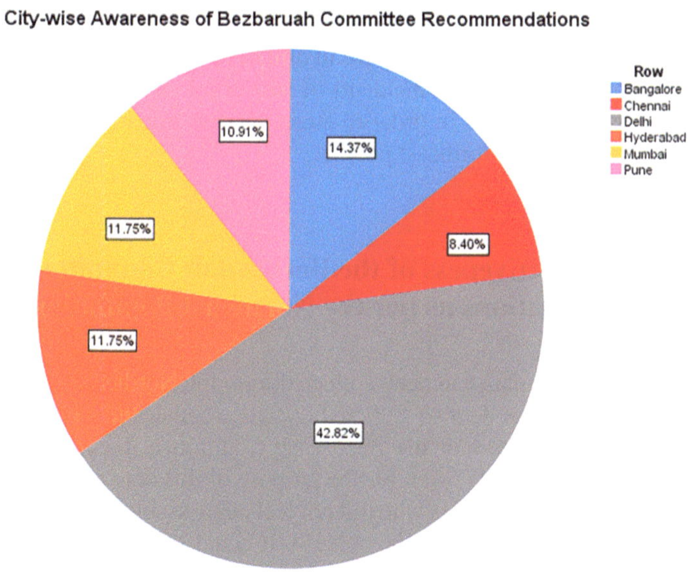

Fig. 5.3 Awareness of Northeast Indians regarding Bezbaruah Committee Recommendations

respondents were taken for the purpose of this data analyzation. In the data, there were such respondents who did not feel comfortable answering the question – which were symbolized by the value 0. In Bangalore, 11.4% of the Northeast people were aware about the said recommendations, and 6.7% of the Northeast people in Chennai, 34% in Delhi, 9.3% in Hyderabad, 9.3% in Mumbai, and 8.7% in Pune were aware of the recommendations. This means to say that most Northeast people from Delhi were aware of the recommendations. On the contrary, 81.9% of the Northeast Indians in Bangalore were not aware of the recommendations, 89.3% in Chennai, 58.7% in Delhi, 84% in Hyderabad, 68.7% in Mumbai, and 80.7% of the Northeast people in Pune were not aware of Bezbaruah Committee Recommendations.

The Bezbaruah Committee was set up in 2014 as an aftermath to the hate crime and death of Nido Taniam, a 19-year-old Northeast Indian. It gave recommendations with regard to various hate crime concerns and was the very first step for the protection of the Northeasterners in India.

5.5.1 Interpretation

It could be observed that Delhi had the most aware Northeast population in this regard. However, it also could be seen that most people in Bangalore and Chennai were not aware of the Bezbaruah Committee Recommendations. For the people to understand the rights that they had fight for, they had to know about what rights they have. Developments like the Bezbaruah Committee Recommendations were made for those sections of the society that were in dire need of an instrument that would grant them extra protection from incidents of hate crime. It was very important to spread awareness of the same in order to attain success in curbing discrimination and hate crime against the Northeast people.

5.6 Faith in Effectiveness of the Bezbaruah Committee Recommendations as per the Northeast Population

In the Figs. 5.4 and 5.5, data had been collected from the Northeast people of India living in metro cities. The data so gathered depicts whether the Northeast Indians had faith in the effectiveness of the Bezbaruah Committee Recommendations. A total of 900 respondents were taken for the purpose of this data analyzation. In the data, there were such respondents who did not feel comfortable answering the question – which were symbolized by the value 0. It could be seen that 10.7% of the Northeast people in Bangalore believe in the effectiveness of the recommendations, and 8% in Chennai, 29.3% in Delhi, 10% in Hyderabad, 10% in Mumbai, and 9.3%

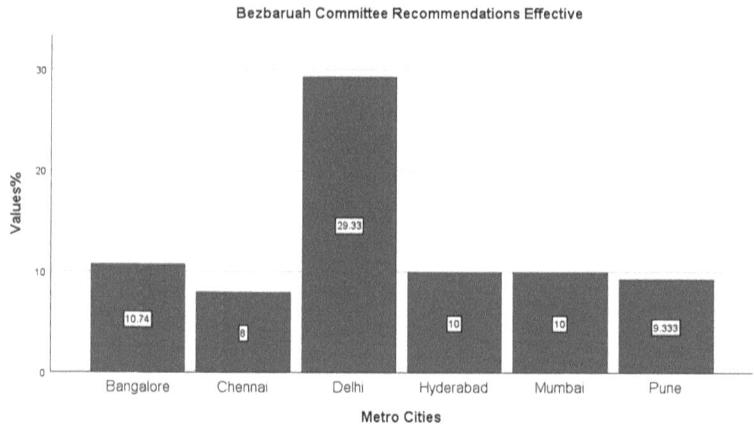

Fig. 5.4 Faith in effectiveness of Bezbaruah Committee Recommendations

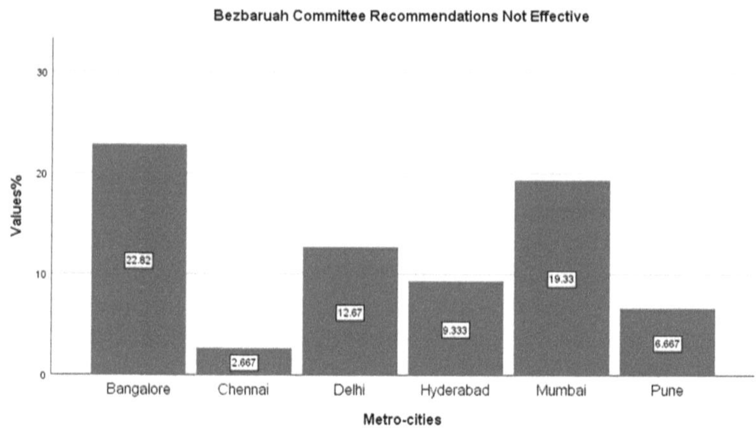

Fig. 5.5 No faith in effectiveness of Bezbaruah Committee Recommendations

in Pune had faith in the effectiveness of the recommendations. On the contrary, 22.8% of the Northeast people in Bangalore believe that these recommendations would be ineffective, and 2.7% in Chennai, 12.7% in Delhi, 9.3% in Hyderabad, 19.3% in Mumbai, and 6.7% in Pune did not have faith in the effectiveness of the Bezbaruah Committee Recommendations.

5.6.1 *Interpretation*

It was observed that Delhi was the metropolitan city where most Northeast Indians had faith that the Bezbaruah Committee Recommendations would be effective in countering incidents of hate crimes against the Northeast Indian people, whereas most Northeastern people in Bangalore believe that these recommendations would be ineffective. This could also because of the reason that as seen from the previous segment, and most people from Delhi were aware of these recommendations. It becomes impossible to encourage people to have faith in these recommendations when they were not aware of the same. Other than that, it could also be said that people suffering from these incidents since a very long time might had certain amount of skepticism regarding successful developments in this area. But that would improve when people would see tangible changes.

5.7 Need for New Laws

In Table 5.1, data with respect to the perception of the Northeast population in metropolitan cities are depicted on the issue whether they believed the new law against hate crime against the Northeast Indians was needed or if the existing laws were sufficient. As could be seen from the data above, most percentage of the Northeast people consider that existing laws should be strengthened in order to deal with the hate crimes, rather than new laws be introduced. In Bangalore, 88.9% of the Northeast people believe that existing laws must be followed, whereas only 11.1% of the Northeast people consider that new laws must be brought in order to reduce the crime. In Chennai, 40.7% of the Northeast people believe that existing laws must be followed, whereas only 59.3% of the Northeast people consider that new laws must be brought in order to reduce the crime. In Delhi, 79.1% of the Northeast people believe that existing laws must be followed, whereas only 20.9% of the Northeast people consider that new laws must be brought in order to reduce the crime. In Hyderabad, 58.3% of the Northeast people believe that existing laws must be followed, whereas only 41.7% of the Northeast people consider that new laws must be brought in order to reduce the crime. In Mumbai, 83.9% of the Northeast people believe that existing laws must be followed, whereas only 16.1% of the Northeast people consider that new laws must be brought in order to reduce the crime. In Pune, 52.6% of the Northeast people believe that existing laws must be followed, whereas only 47.4% of the Northeast people consider that new laws must

Table 5.1 City-wise distribution of Northeast people suggesting on the need for new law

City-wise suggestions by N-E people	Existing law followed		New stricter laws, policies, and agencies		Total	
	N	Percentage	N	Percentage	N	Percentage
Bangalore	16	88.9	2	11.1	18	100.0
Chennai	11	40.7	16	59.3	27	100.0
Delhi	34	79.1	9	20.9	43	100.0
Hyderabad	7	58.3	5	41.7	12	100.0
Mumbai	26	83.9	5	16.1	31	100.0
Pune	10	52.6	9	47.4	19	100.0

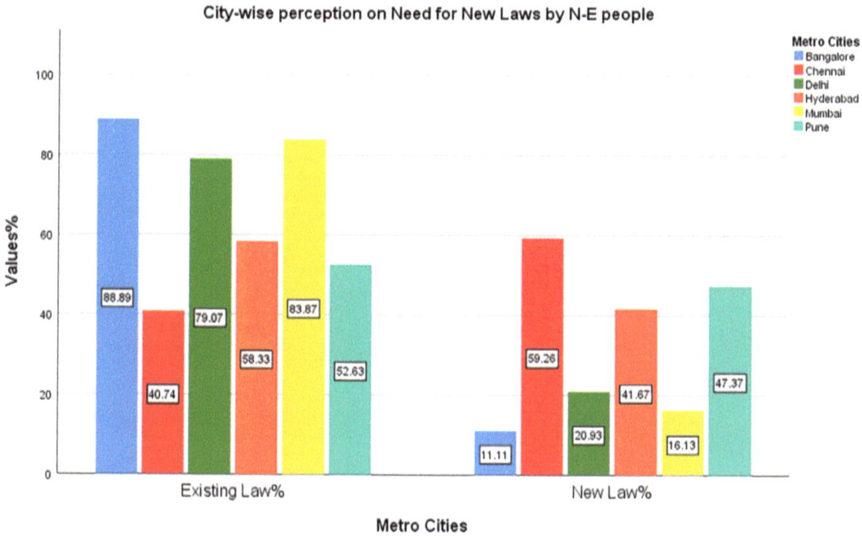

Fig. 5.6 City-wise perception on the need for new law by Northeast people

be brought in order to reduce the crime. The same data has been instituted in graphical form in Fig. 5.6.

5.7.1 Interpretation

From the above statistical information, researchers could clearly deduce that Bangalore was the city where most Northeast people did not consider that new law should be instituted, rather they preferred existing laws to be implemented and executed in the right manner so as to curb the crime. Whereas a greater percentage of the Northeast population in Chennai believed that a new law was the solution to hate crimes. On an average, most people seemed to perceive that new law could not be a viable solution to this crime. The reasons to believe that existing laws could solve the crime of hate crime against the Northeast Indians could be multiple. Enacting and implementing new law had its own set of problems. It takes a lot of effort, extra infrastructure, and more time for a new law to reach the masses and show a positive effect for the Northeast Indians. It becomes easier for existing laws to be implemented by bringing adequate amendments to solve the current problem of hate crimes against the Northeast people if required. Also, according to many respondents, new laws mean giving special or differential treatment to the Northeast people. This section of the population already suffers through much alienation and a certain level of exclusion by the society; new law may only aggravate the situation.

Chapter 6
Findings and Suggestions

6.1 Introduction

In the present study on Hate Crime in India: Understanding Nuances Discrimination Against Northeastern Population, this chapter represents the penultimate segment of this book. Through this section, the authors aim to discuss the key findings of the study conducted. It entails key variable findings, discussions, and suggestions. The key variable findings of the chapter review the variables that had been studied in the previous chapters as its research questions. These findings discuss and interpret the research question as mentioned in Chap. 1. Discussions to the study include where the authors had explored the hypothesis of the research. Suggestions analyze the suggestive measures as gathered from the empirical study and enumerate further preventive and corrective steps on behalf of the authors.

6.2 Key Variable Findings

- From Chap. 2 of this book, the authors were able to deduce the profile of the Northeast Indian respondents that had been taken into consideration for the current study. In Bangalore, most respondents were male (54%), from the age group of 23–30 years (46.7%); Chennai mostly had male respondents (55.3%) from the age group of 23–30 years (76.7%); Delhi mostly had female respondents (51.3%) from the age group of 18–22 years (50.7%); Hyderabad had female respondents (52.7%) from the age group of 23–30 years (48.7%); Mumbai mostly had female respondents (55.3%) from the age group of 23–30 years (62.7%); and Pune mostly had female respondents (52%) from the age group of 23–30 years (52%). To sum it up, mostly the respondents residing across all the six cities were in the age group of 23–30 years (female population more dominant compared to males).

G. S. Bajpai et al., *Hate Crime in India*,
https://doi.org/10.1007/978-3-031-30522-1_6

- Chapter 3 discussed two aspects: – prejudices which the Northeast people suffered from and the security concerns or violence faced by them.
  - Prejudices were divided into three parts based on geographical difference, cultural difference, and physical appearance. Most Northeast Indian respondents who faced geographical difference as the reason for prejudice were from Mumbai (32.7%).

    The general population who believed that geographical difference was the underlying reason for prejudice against the Northeast people hailed from Mumbai (42%); most of the Northeast respondents facing prejudice due to cultural difference were from Mumbai (62.7%), and most of the general population believing that cultural difference was the reason for prejudice were from Mumbai (66%); most of the Northeast respondents suffering prejudices based on physical appearance were from Chennai (58%), and most of the general population considering physical appearance to be the reason of prejudice were from Mumbai (78%).
  - To analyze security concerns and violence against the Northeast Indians, the hate crime incidents encountered and witnessed were considered. Most Northeasterners encountered hate crime incidents in Mumbai (44.7%), and most Northeasterners who witnessed the crime to have happened with fellow Northeast Indians were reported in Chennai (66%). The general population who witnessed hate crime incidents against the Northeast Indians was reported in Delhi (66%).
  - Among the type of hate crime incidents, offensive and abusive language used against the Northeast Indians was common across all six states: Bangalore (43.3%), Chennai (72%), Delhi (64%), Hyderabad (48.7%), Mumbai (74%), and Pune (67.3%). The most prevalent reasons behind hate crime incidents against the Northeast Indians identified as per our data analysis were public attitude and insensitivity. This was quite common in Bangalore (17.4%). Lack of awareness and knowledge in Chennai (21.3%), public attitude and insensitivity in Delhi (24%), public attitude and insensitivity in Hyderabad (12.7%), physical appearance and ethnicity in Mumbai (18.7%), and physical appearance and ethnicity in Pune (11.3%) were identified. During such violence/humiliation at the time of hate crime incidents, mental status of the victims was recorded to be most disrupted in Delhi as afraid and unsafe (17.3%), followed by Bangalore (16.7%).

- Chapter 4 covered important facets of the Hate Crime in India: Understanding Nuances Discrimination Against the Northeastern Population that included reporting of the crime to the police, police approach, police treatment, and secondary victimization.
  - As a consequence of hate crime, most Northeast Indians avoided reporting of the incidences rather than taking action (32.3%), with more in Chennai than other cities (8.2%). The reason for such heavy non-reporting according to the Northeast Indians in Bangalore as per the data collected that the Northeast

Indians in this city had accepted the treatment that was given to them and chose to helplessly ignore for a hassle-free living (15.3%). In Chennai, the police were not serious toward hate crime incidents against the Northeasterners (14%). In Delhi, the seriousness of the police toward such incidents was recorded to be (20.1%). In Hyderabad, there was a similar situation like Bangalore; they accepted the treatment and chose to ignore (12.7%). In Mumbai, it was recorded to be 26%, and in Pune, behavior of the people toward the seriousness of this issue was recorded to be 14%. Among the people who preferred to report the incident to the police (11.5%) and those who did not (71.5), most people residing in Bangalore City avoided approaching the police (79.9%), while in Delhi, approaching the police to report was recorded to be 11.5%.

- In the event of the hate crime incident being reported, most Northeasterners faced a common issue across all six metro cities regarding refusal to file FIR by the police. It was recorded as follows: Bangalore (6%), Chennai (2%), Delhi (4%), Hyderabad (0.7%), Pune (4%), and Mumbai (2%). It was also observed that the police weren't ready to consider any such person as a victim of hate crime in Mumbai. It was pertinent to note that the percentage where the police were mostly understanding and considerate toward such victims – Bangalore (6%), Chennai (5.3%), Delhi (6%), and Pune (6.7%) – on the other hand, as per the data collected by the authors it showed less percentage of misbehavior faced by the Northeast population by the police in Hyderabad (2%) and Mumbai (4%).
- Due to hate crime incidents against the Northeast people being a common practice in our society, the Northeast people residing in Chennai who were afraid of living in the metro city were recorded to be 34%, followed by those in Mumbai (7.3%), who were often worried staying in the metro city, and Hyderabad, who were recorded to be 15.3%.
- Northeasterners living in Chennai were reported to be the most afraid of being subjected to hate crime incidents due to their identity (74%).

• Chapter 5 enunciated the legal connotation to hate crime incidents against the Northeastern population of the country.

  - From the data collected on the point of existing laws being adequate to curb such incidents, it was deduced that most Northeast Indian respondents who believed that the laws were adequate was reported from Delhi (24.7%), most people who believed that existing laws were adequate only with better implementation were from Hyderabad (14%), and most people who believed that the existing laws were not adequate were reported from Chennai (24.7%).
  - Among the general population respondents, most people believing that existing laws were adequate resided in Delhi (78%) and most people believing that they were inadequate reported from Chennai (68%).
  - When it came to recommendations given by the Bezbaruah Committee, most Northeasterners in Delhi considered them to be effective (29.3%), and most Northeasterners in Bangalore considered them to be ineffective (22.8%).

- On the question whether there was a need for new laws to curb hate crime incidents against the Northeast Indians, most percentages of Northeasterners in Bangalore believed that the existing laws were quite sufficient and there wasn't any need of new Law (88.9%); however, in Chennai, the Northeasterners pressed toward the need for new laws (59.3%).

6.3 Discussions

This segment focusses on the final analysis of hypothesis testing in the book. There were two hypotheses studied by the authors, i.e., geographical indifference, physical appearance, and cultural difference had led to an increase in prejudicial attitude against the Northeast people residing in metro cities. Further, dearth of legal protection toward Northeast people had led to an increase in hate crime incidences. Following were the final deductions inferred from the testing done in Chaps. 3 and 4:

1. *Hypothesis 1* (part of Chap. 3) took into account the relationship between the three reasons for prejudices against the Northeast Indians with the attitude of the police that they were subjected to in the event of a hate crime incident being committed. This testing was conducted using the Chi-square method. The authors concluded that there wasn't enough evidence to suggest an association between geographical and cultural difference and police treatment in handling the Northeast people suffering from any kind of violence; however, there was enough evidence to suggest an association between physical appearance and police treatment in handling the Northeast people suffering from any kind of violence. This goes to say reasons of prejudices like geographical difference and the cultural difference did not influence prejudicial treatment by the police, but the physical appearance of the Northeastern population of the country determined the treatment that the Northeasterners received from the police in the event of the occurrence of hate crime incident.
2. *Hypothesis 2* (part of Chap. 4) took into account the correlation between hate crime incidents against the Northeast Indians and the adequacy of laws against such incidents. This testing was conducted by way of correlation analysis between the two variables. It deduced that the direction of the relationship was a weak positive correlation (i.e., adequacy of laws and hate crime incidents were positively correlated). This means that these variables tend to increase together; in other words, where hate crime incidents increased, it led to increase in the view that existing laws were inadequate. Conversely, if belief in existing laws to be inadequate increased, it was directly and positively correlated with an increase in hate crime incidents against the Northeast Indians.

6.4 Suggestions

During the study on Hate Crime in India, authors came across various aspects of hate crime which had traumatized the Northeasterners in India. Suggestions by the Northeast population as well as the general population were also taken into consideration as they are the main target group of the study. Based on the findings, responses, and case studies accumulated and analyzed by the authors, the following suggestive measures were identified:

1. AICC-Centre for North-East Relations (AICC-CNER) had introduced a separate helpline for the Northeast people in the year 2014. However, seeing the statistics, it was evident that the helpline was not effective and known to people. The initiative had to be taken to sensitize people about this helpline.
2. Appointing of a Northeast operator who could deal with the grievances of the Northeast people approach the helpline. This would also provide employment opportunities to the Northeast people.
3. Collection of accurate data on hate crimes was very limited to government bodies like AICC-CNER, Ministry of Home Affairs (MHA), and the police. It would be more fruitful if the government bodies involve academicians as well those who specifically work in the field of social issues.
4. Appointing of competent police officials, especially in the lower-grade level, who must be fluent enough to interact with the victims of such crimes.
5. Designing an operational guide for police, as well as formulating guidelines for handling of victims and witnesses of hate crime, investigation process, and prosecution of cases, reference of which could be taken from countries like the United Kingdom.
6. Training police officials, especially the constables, to ensure sensitive treatment toward the victims.
7. Establishing NGOs specifically working toward rehabilitating and restoring victims of hate crime.
8. Ensuring effective implementation of existing legal provisions for protection against hate crime and hate speech in Indian Penal Code, where the bias or hate motive could act as a punishment enhancer.
9. Need for legally defining the term "hate crime" according to the Indian Constitution and prevailing social conditions.
10. Center for the Northeast people in every district as well as student bodies in every university and college, which would consist of social workers, psychologists, and legal personnel. These people would be the first encounter group to the Northeast victims of hate crime.
11. The center/committee/student bodies need to have an official statutory character. It has been 9 years since the Bezbaruah Committee submitted its findings; there is a need to reconstitute such a committee, especially when COVID-19 is being termed as China virus as a consequence of which the Northeasterners are facing the brunt of violence.

12. The committee which will be formulated should consist of members of the Northeastern section of the society and female participants. The same should be implemented across all the student bodies of educational institutions.
13. Sensitizing of the community and fostering relationship between law enforcement and community groups. This would restore the Northeast people to their faith in law and justice. It would enable them to confidently report hate crimes.
14. Educating people, especially children from a very early age, about the concept of "hate crimes." Refurbishing the school curriculum to make children aware of the social issues around them.

In the above Table 6.1, data collated responses from the Northeast Indian population to curb hate crime incidents against them in metro cities.

Table 6.1 Suggestions by the Northeast population

Suggestions by the Northeasterners in metro cities		N	Percentage
Bangalore	0	61	40.7
	Equality	18	12.0
	Changing perception	13	8.7
	Knowledge and awareness	18	12.0
	Public proactiveness	2	1.3
	Existing law followed	16	10.7
	New stricter laws, policies, and agencies	2	1.3
	No solution exists	14	9.3
	Not sure	6	4.0
	Total	150	100.0
Chennai	0	51	34.0
	Equality	15	10.0
	Changing perception	15	10.0
	Knowledge and awareness	37	24.7
	Public proactiveness	1	0.7
	Existing law followed	11	7.3
	New stricter laws, policies, and agencies	16	10.7
	No solution exists	3	2.0
	Not sure	1	0.7
	Total	150	100.0
Delhi	0	33	22.0
	Equality	2	1.3
	Changing perception	23	15.3
	Knowledge and awareness	43	28.7
	Public proactiveness	2	1.3
	Existing law followed	34	22.7
	New stricter laws, policies, and agencies	9	6.0
	No solution exists	0	0.0
	Not sure	4	2.7
	Total	150	100.0

(continued)

Table 6.1 (continued)

Suggestions by the Northeasterners in metro cities		N	Percentage
Hyderabad	0	80	53.3
	Equality	3	2.0
	Changing perception	11	7.3
	Knowledge and awareness	36	24.0
	Public proactiveness	1	0.7
	Existing law followed	7	4.7
	New stricter laws, policies, and agencies	5	3.3
	No solution exists	5	3.3
	Not sure	2	1.3
	Total	150	100.0
Mumbai	0	59	39.3
	Equality	6	4.0
	Changing perception	10	6.7
	Knowledge and awareness	41	27.3
	Public proactiveness	0	0.0
	Existing law followed	26	17.3
	New stricter laws, policies, and agencies	5	3.3
	No solution exists	3	2.0
	Not sure	0	0.0
	Total	150	100.0
Pune	0	84	56.0
	Equality	7	4.7
	Changing perception	13	8.7
	Knowledge and awareness	22	14.7
	Public proactiveness	3	2.0
	Existing law followed	10	6.7
	New stricter laws, policies, and agencies	9	6.0
	No solution exists	2	1.3
	Not sure	0	0.0
	Total	150	100.0

6.4.1 Explanation

(i) In Bangalore, 12% of the Northeast Indians responded by saying promoting equality among the people would help curb hate crimes in the city; 8.7% of the Northeast people believed that steps to change the perception of the population in a metro city would be effective; 12% suggested that instilling knowledge and awareness could be key to decrease the hate crimes; 1.3% perceived that public proactiveness in promoting ill-consequences to hate crime could act as a support in making people aware; 10.7% of the respondents believed that existing laws should be followed stringently; 1.3% suggested that new stricter laws, policies, and agencies should be brought into practice; and 9.3% did not believe that there was any solution against this crime.

(ii) In Chennai, 10% of the Northeast Indians responded by saying promoting equality among the people would help curb hate crimes in the city; 10% of the Northeasterners believed that steps to change the perception of the population in a metro city would be effective, 24.7% suggested that instilling knowledge and awareness would be key to decrease the hate crimes; 0.7% perceived that public proactiveness in promoting ill-consequences to hate crime would act as a support in making people aware; 7.3% of the respondents believed that existing laws should be followed stringently; 10.7% suggested that new stricter laws, policies, and agencies should be brought into practice; and 2% did not believe that there was any solution against this crime.

(iii) In Delhi, 1.3% of the Northeast Indians responded by saying promoting equality among the people would help curb hate crimes in the city, 15.3% of the Northeasterners believed that steps to change the perception of the population in a metro city would be effective; 28.7% suggested that instilling knowledge and awareness could be key to decrease the hate crimes; 1.3% perceived that public proactiveness in promoting ill-consequences to hate crime would act as a support in making people aware; 22.7% of the respondents believed that existing laws should be followed stringently; 6% suggested that new stricter laws, policies, and agencies should be brought into practice; and 0.0% did not believe that there was any solution against this crime.

(iv) In Hyderabad, 2% of the Northeast Indians responded by saying promoting equality among the people would help curb hate crimes in the city; 7.3% of the Northeasterners believed that steps to change the perception of the population in a metro city would be effective; 24% suggested that instilling knowledge and awareness would be key to decrease the hate crimes; 0.7% perceived that public proactiveness in promoting ill-consequences to hate crime would act as a support in making people aware; 4.7% of the respondents believed that existing laws should be followed stringently; 3.3% suggested that new stricter laws, policies, and agencies should be brought into practice; and 3.3% do not believe that there was any solution against this crime.

(v) In Mumbai, 4% of the Northeast Indians responded by saying promoting equality among the people would help curb hate crimes in the city; 6.7% of the Northeasterners believed that steps to change the perception of the population in a metro city would be effective; 27.3% suggested that instilling knowledge and awareness could be key to decrease the hate crimes; 0.0% perceived that public proactiveness in promoting ill-consequences to hate crime would act as a support in making people aware; 17.3% of the respondents believed that existing laws should be followed stringently; 3.3% suggested that new stricter laws, policies, and agencies should be brought into practice; and 2% did not believe that there was any solution against this crime.

(vi) In Pune, 4.7% of the Northeast Indians responded by saying promoting equality among the people would help curb hate crimes in the city; 8.7% of the Northeasterners believed that steps to change the perception of the population in a metro city would be effective; 14.7% suggested that instilling knowledge and awareness would be key to decrease the hate crimes; 2% perceived that public proactiveness in promoting ill-consequences to hate crime would act as a support in making people aware; 6.7% of the respondents believed that existing laws should be followed stringently; 6% suggested that new stricter laws, policies and agencies should be brought into practice; and 1.3% did not believe that there was any solution against this crime.

In Table 6.2 are data accumulated responses from the general population in order to curb hate crimes incidents against the Northeast Indian population residing in metro cities.

Table 6.2 Suggestions by the general people

Suggestions by the general people in metro cities		N	Percentage
Bangalore	0	28	56.0
	Equality	6	12.0
	Changing perception	6	12.0
	Knowledge and awareness	4	8.0
	Public proactiveness	1	2.0
	Existing law followed properly	1	2.0
	New stricter laws, policies, and agencies	2	4.0
	No solution exists	1	2.0
	Not sure	1	2.0
	Total	50	100.0
Chennai	0	9	18.0
	Equality	3	6.0
	Changing perception	4	8.0
	Knowledge and awareness	6	12.0
	Public proactiveness	1	2.0
	Existing law followed	6	12.0
	New stricter laws, policies, and agencies	18	36.0
	No solution exists	2	4.0
	Not sure	1	2.0
	Total	50	100.0
Delhi	0	10	20.0
	Equality	6	12.0
	Changing perception	10	20.0
	Knowledge and awareness	11	22.0
	Public proactiveness	0	0.0
	Existing law followed	3	6.0
	New stricter laws, policies, and agencies	10	20.0
	No solution exists	0	0.0
	Not sure	0	0.0
	Total	50	100.0

(continued)

Table 6.2 (continued)

Suggestions by the general people in metro cities		N	Percentage
Hyderabad	0	24	48.0
	Equality	3	6.0
	Changing perception	5	10.0
	Knowledge and awareness	5	10.0
	Public proactiveness	2	4.0
	Existing law followed	7	14.0
	New stricter laws, policies, and agencies	3	6.0
	No solution exists	1	2.0
	Not sure	0	0.0
	Total	50	100.0
Mumbai	0	24	48.0
	Equality	2	4.0
	Changing perception	8	16.0
	Knowledge and awareness	14	28.0
	Public proactiveness	1	2.0
	Existing law followed	0	0.0
	New stricter laws, policies, and agencies	1	2.0
	No solution exists	0	0.0
	Not sure	0	0.0
	Total	50	100.0
Pune	0	32	64.0
	Equality	4	8.0
	Changing perception	5	10.0
	Knowledge and awareness	3	6.0
	Public proactiveness	1	2.0
	Existing law followed properly	1	2.0
	New stricter laws, policies, and agencies	2	4.0
	No solution exists	1	2.0
	Not sure	1	2.0
	Total	50	100.0

6.4.2 *Explanation*

(i) In Bangalore, 12% of the general people responded by saying promoting equality among the people would help curb hate crimes in the city; 12% of the Northeasterners believed that steps to change the perception of the population in a metro city would be effective; 8% suggested that instilling knowledge and awareness could be key to decrease the hate crimes; 2% perceived that public proactiveness in promoting ill-consequences to hate crime would act as a support in making people aware; 2% of the respondents believed that existing laws should be followed stringently; 4% suggested that new stricter laws, policies, and agencies should be brought into practice; and 2% did not believe that there was any solution against this crime.

(ii) In Chennai, 6% of the general population responded by saying promoting equality among the people would help curb hate crimes in the city; 8% of the Northeasterners believed that steps to change the perception of the population in a metro city would be effective; 12% suggested that instilling knowledge and awareness could be key to decreasing the hate crimes; 2% perceived that public proactiveness in promoting ill-consequences to hate crime would act as a support in making people aware; 12% of the respondents believed that existing laws should be followed stringently; 36% suggested that new stricter laws, policies, and agencies should be brought into practice; and 4% did not believe that there was any solution against this crime.

(iii) In Delhi, 12% of the general population responded by saying promoting equality among the people would help curb hate crimes in the city; 20% of the Northeasterners believed that steps to change the perception of the population in a metro city would be effective; 22% suggested that instilling knowledge and awareness could be key to decrease the hate crimes; 0.0% perceived that public proactiveness in promoting ill-consequences to hate crime would act as a support in making people aware; 6% of the respondents believed that existing laws should be followed stringently; 20% suggested that new stricter laws, policies, and agencies should be brought into practice; and 0.0% did not believe that there was any solution against this crime.

(iv) In Hyderabad, 6% of the general population responded by saying promoting equality among the people would help curb hate crimes in the city; 10% of the Northeasterners believed that steps to change the perception of the population in a metro city would be effective; 10% suggested that instilling knowledge and awareness would be key to decrease the hate crimes; 4% perceived that public proactiveness in promoting ill-consequences to hate crime would act as a support in making people aware; 14% of the respondents believed that existing laws should be followed stringently; 6% suggested that new stricter laws, policies, and agencies should be brought into practice; and 2% did not believe that there was any solution against this crime.

(v) In Mumbai, 4% of the general population responded by saying promoting equality among the people would help curb hate crimes in the city; 16% of the Northeasterners believed that steps to change the perception of the population in a metro city would be effective; 28% suggested that instilling knowledge and awareness could be key to decrease the hate crimes; 2% perceived that public proactiveness in promoting ill-consequences to hate crime would act as a support in making people aware; 0.0% of the respondents believed that existing laws should be followed stringently; 2% suggested that new stricter laws, policies, and agencies should be brought into practice; and 0.0% did not believe that there was any solution against this crime.

(vi) In Pune, 4.7% of the general population responded by saying promoting equality among the people would help curb hate crimes in the city; 8% of the Northeasterners believed that steps to change the perception of the population in a metro city would be effective; 10% suggested that instilling knowledge and awareness would be key to decrease the hate crimes; 6% perceived that public proactiveness in promoting ill-consequences to hate crime would act as a support in making people aware; 2% of the respondents believed that existing laws should be followed stringently; 4% suggested that new stricter laws, policies, and agencies should be brought into practice; and 2% did not believe that there was any solution against this crime.

(vii) Increasing knowledge capacity among the general people by organizing official government-led awareness camps. These awareness camps could include various interactive activities and promote communication on an intercommunity and inter-race level.

(viii) Print media and multimedia in the form of newspapers, radios, and television could be utilized to broadcast and disseminate awareness advertisements and advisories by the government in order to make the message of solidarity and sensitivity reach every household in every way.

Chapter 7
Summary and Conclusion

7.1 Summary

The book addressed the growing trend of cases related to prejudice and violence against the people of the Northeast regions of India, forming what we may call hate crimes. This book aimed to understand the various prejudices associated with hate crimes through the experiences of the Northeast people residing in six metro cities – Delhi, Mumbai, Bangalore, Pune, Chennai, and Hyderabad. Furthermore, it also studied whether the existing laws were sufficient to cater to the needs of the Northeast people or if there was a need for a new law on hate crimes. The Northeast people and the general population residing in six metropolitan cities were selected as the target group for data collection. Case studies were also taken for a detailed understanding of the subject in question. For this purpose, the objectives of the research project were summarized as follows:

- To study the profile of people from the Northeast residing in metropolitan cities like Delhi, Mumbai, Hyderabad, Pune, Chennai, and Bangalore
- To examine the various kinds of security concerns and experiences faced in the daily life of the Northeastern people while residing in metro cities
- To identify reasons behind the acts of prejudice and violence (hate crimes) against the people from the Northeast
- To understand the nature of secondary victimization faced by the Northeastern people during post-victimization stages
- To critically evaluate the existing legal framework's effectiveness in comprehensively dealing with cases of prejudices and violence faced by people from the Northeastern states
- To suggest preventive measures for minimizing the concerns that law enforcement agencies could take

G. S. Bajpai et al., *Hate Crime in India*,
https://doi.org/10.1007/978-3-031-30522-1_7

A pilot survey was done before the actual study to gain better insight into the problem. Pursuantly, pretesting was done by the team. Selection of the Northeastern population was based on the *purposive sampling technique*, as the study was concerned with only Northeastern people. The individual sample was identified using the *snowball sampling technique* to build rapport and connect easily to get accurate information. A total of 1200 respondents participated, i.e., 200 respondents from each metro city.

- For data analysis and interpretation, the research team used SPSS software. The book was divided into seven chapters: Chap. 1 covered the Introduction, Literature Review, Statement of the Problem, and Research Methodology. Chapter 2 analyzed the profiles of the Northeast population of India along with the general population living in metropolitan cities. Chapter 3 examined the rationale behind security concerns about hate crimes. The research team also tested the hypothesis formulated in Chap. 1 using advanced statistical methods. This led to the conclusion that physical appearance was a dominant variable leading to increased prejudicial attitudes against the Northeast people residing in metro cities compared to the variables of geographical difference and cultural difference. Chapter 4 covered the secondary victimization faced by the Northeast people during the post-victimization stages. It also captured the experiences of the general population (if anyone in their proximity had been a part of/had faced any discrimination). The second half of Chap. 4 tested the second hypothesis of Chap. 1 and found that adequacies of existing laws and hate crime incidents had a statistically significant linear relationship, thus concluding that these variables tend to increase together. Chapter 5 assessed the legal developments and services provided against hate crimes to the Northeast population. It further covered the extent of awareness among the people related to the laws. Finally, Chap. 6 highlighted the research project's key findings and suggestions by the research team.

7.1.1 Major Key Findings

- Most Northeast Indian respondents who faced geographical difference as the reason for prejudice were from Mumbai (32.7%); most Northeast respondents facing prejudice due to cultural difference were from Mumbai (62.7%); and most Northeast respondents suffering prejudices based on physical appearance were from Chennai (58%).
- Most Northeasterners encountered hate crime incidents in Mumbai (44.7%), and most Northeasterners witnessed the crime to have happened with fellow Northeast Indians in Chennai (66%).
- Among the type of hate crime incidents, offensive and abusive language used against the Northeast Indians was most common across all six states, i.e., Bangalore (43.3%), Chennai (72%), Delhi (64%), Hyderabad (48.7%), Mumbai (74%), and Pune (67.3%). The most prevalent reasons behind hate crime

incidents against the Northeast Indians identified as per our data analysis were public attitude and insensitivity. This was quite common in Bangalore.

- When the hate crime incident was reported, most Northeasterners faced a common issue of refusal to file an FIR by the police.
- Northeast people residing in Chennai who were afraid of living in the metro city recorded (34%).
- Northeasterners living in Chennai reported being most afraid of hate crime incidents due to their identity (74%).
- From the data collected on the point of existing laws being adequate to curb such incidents, it was deduced that most Northeast Indian respondents who believe that they were adequate reported from Delhi (24.7%).
- On the question of whether there was a need for a new law to curb hate crime incidents against Northeast Indians, most Northeasterners in Bangalore believed that the existing laws were sufficient, and there wasn't any need for a new law (88.9%). However, in Chennai, the Northeasterners pressed for a new law (59.3%).

This chapter summarized the whole research along with the conclusion. Additionally, there is a Bibliography and Annexures with interview schedules and case studies.

This book was thus an effort to map the experiences and vulnerabilities of people of the Northeast regions in metro cities in their interaction with educational institutions and workplaces.

7.2 Conclusion

This book, through the empirical data collected across six metro cities, highlighted many incidents of hate crime faced by the Northeast people. Through the suggestions formulated after analyzing the data and observing the target group, the researchers pointed out that a comprehensive effort had to be made to avoid discrimination based on racial and geographical indifference. Strategical planning by formulating programs and initiatives by the government would help control the prejudices associated with hate crimes. Further, cooperation by the general population was the need of the hour. The book has tried to capture the everyday experiences and identify the challenges of the Northeast people residing in six metro cities. While collecting the data, it came to the research team's knowledge that people were not even aware of the existence of the Northeastern states within India. Lack of knowledge about the laws and the rights of the Northeast people and the handling of the victims of hate crimes was also an eye-opener for the team. In other words, people need to understand that the Northeast region was part of India, and any kind of discrimination or disrespect toward the people of the Northeast was a violation of their fundamental and constitutional rights. A broad mindset coupled with the right education could act as a foundation to make people aware and recognize the Northeast people as their fellow citizens. Ultimately, it was our responsibility to introspect on how we look toward the people of the Northeast. The book was thus an attempt to understand the plight of the Northeast people, how law enforcement agencies handled the cases of hate crime incidents, and whether the existing laws were sufficient to cater to the needs of the Northeast population.

Annexures

Annexure 1: Case Study Analysis

Case study method involves investigating contemporary phenomena within its real-life context. The boundaries between the phenomena which was studied and the real-life instance that was discussed are not differentiated particularly; both are merged in a way to support each other. Case study method deals with the "how" and "why" of any issue that needs in-depth analysis. Researchers had no control over the variables in the case study research method, and so, the method of replication was followed in the current study where common variables are located and compared so as to derive an analysis.

There were two methods by which case study research is conducted:

- Holistic case study method – wherein case studies are examined holistically or as one unit summarily
- Embedded case study method – where case studies were examined as subunits and then were put to analysis, linking the case studies to the main issue of the research

In the current study, the researchers had used embedded case study method.

Case Study 1 (Bangalore)

In the city of Bangalore, Y, a 32-year-old northeastern man from Arunachal Pradesh, aspired to start a merchandise shop near a bustling colony. He contacted another man who could rent him the infrastructure to start his business. He paid the rent in full; however, he did not expect that the owner would ask him to vacate the premises instead. There was no concrete or reasonable explanation that the owner gave; moreover, he

G. S. Bajpai et al., *Hate Crime in India*,
https://doi.org/10.1007/978-3-031-30522-1

refused to return the payment to Y also. Upon trying to reason with the owner, the owner physically assaulted Y, continuously addressing him by the name "bloody chinky." Aggrieved by this incident, Y reported the matter in 2017, to which the Police officials were very supportive. First hearing took place on March 2018 in which the owner did not turn up because he was out of India at that time. There was no appearance in court in the second hearing as well which was on October 2018. Later, the owner communicated that he was willing to settle the matter by way of compromise instead. Y, already given his best efforts in redressing his grievance, took the option for a compromise and settled for the meager amount he received from the owner.

The aforementioned incident could be safely put under the acts included in hate crime. This was for the apparent reason that Y was caused monetary and physical harm because he belonged to the Northeastern region of India. This could be seen from the fact that he was being called "bloody chinky" while he was being physically assaulted. This was how any criminal act was differentiated from an act under hate crime when there was presence of bias or hate or some form of differential treatment as one of the key elements.

Analysis

From the case study discussed above, one evident deduction that could be made was being a person from Northeast part of India had made Y to cost and suffer. Taking note of the monetary damage and physical damage, the mental harassment suffered by him was unaccountable and intangible. Even though he received compensation from the owner (perpetrator of the crime), the amount does not suffice or cover the cumulative loss that he had incurred. The payment paid in the beginning as rent, the cost of treatment for the wounds acquired from the physical assault, the cost of litigation, and the future losses that he had suffered from for not being able to run his business as desired could not be embodied in the compensation given. The reason for Y to resort to settling for compensation was that he had lost faith in the judicial redressal mechanism. Even though the case was instituted, there was no development since the owner never appeared before the court. The owner was willing for out-of-court settlement because he wanted this matter to be over; there was no empathy toward the situation of Y. As a consequence to lack of specialized preventive measures and protective procedures for the Northeastern population of India, they were continuously being subjected to injustice and oppression. A mechanism designed specifically to function in such cases would restore faith of the Northeastern people.

Case Study 2 (Bangalore)

Bangalore Metropolitan Transport Corporation (BMTC) was a well-established mechanism of public transportation system since 1997. It was a respite for the public of Bengaluru to have such a service at their disposal. Q was a man in his 60s hailing from Meghalaya. Q had worked in Bangalore for half of his life and had commuted through the bus service. After conversating with the field investigator, he shared his mixed feelings with regard to the environment of the city where he lived and worked. Although he appreciated the work culture and the progress he had made over the years career wise, he merely had a social circle apart from other Northeastern people in the city. The experience iterated to the researcher was of his commute in the public transportation. According to him, people become conscious when he enters a public area especially a public transportation like the bus. Q had lived in Bengaluru for a long time and was aware of the languages of the city like Kannada, Hindi, and English. However, he had come across many young people who make fun of his face and his identity while travelling. These people had ridiculed him on his face, assuming the fact that he would not understand the language. One time when he was travelling with his son, few people humiliated both of them to such an extent that it became a public spectacle. He had been the victim of name-calling and humiliation frequently while living in the city. And after that day, Q preferred that his son does not travel with him and advised his son to take private transportation instead.

Analysis

The above example of Q was a sad state of affairs that the Northeastern people were going through in the city. These actions had deep psychological effects on the Northeastern population residing in the city. As could be seen from the above case study, Q resorted to ignoring the above incident and such incidents that had taken place in the past. Apart from that, the younger generation were receiving similar lesson from these incidents. Hate crimes, such as name-calling because of the identity these northeast Indians belong to, were independent of the victim's individual identity. They were targeted because of their group identity, which was why even the younger generation were the victim of this crime. The unfortunate part was that there was little relief to this population since there were fewer safeguards for protection. This calls for emergent attention to the incidents that go unnoticed.

Case Study 3 (Chennai)

Traffic rules were essential protective guidelines which function with the sole purpose of safeguarding individuals, pedestrians and otherwise, by way of ensuring that certain laws were adhered to while commuting on the road. Traffic police were the agents of the government that were given the duty to oversee that these laws were followed. The problem arises when these traffic rules were arbitrarily used as a tool to harass Northeastern people by the traffic police officers. W, a Northeast Indian male from Mizoram, commutes daily on his motorbike from his place of residence to the place where he works. On one of the days to his work, he forgot his helmet at home and was thereby caught by the traffic police officers for violating the appropriate code of conduct of wearing a helmet while riding a two-wheeler. As a consequence, his license was checked, a challan was issued, and his bike number was noted by the traffic police. At the time when his license was being checked, the traffic police questioned if Mizoram was a place in India. He was continuously interrogated if he was from outside India since they did not believe that "Mizoram" was a state in India. However, after long deliberations and questions, he was allowed to continue to his destination. Being a law-abiding citizen, he fulfilled on his penalty issued by the traffic police officer, but the problem started from the day after the first day when he was stopped. For the next several days, whenever his bike number would come under view of the traffic police officer, he was stopped and was harassed by further questioning regarding his ethnicity, place of dwelling, place of current residence, and information about his bike. He was even asked to pay cash in lieu of the so-called discrepancies that the traffic police had noted in W's answers. At last, being troubled by the traffic police officers frequently, he had to change his usual place of route to his office.

W was repeatedly interrogated by the traffic police officers on account of his ethnicity and the region to which he belonged from in India. This kind of differential, discriminative, and biased treatment indicates how Northeastern people were perceived by the rest of the people and to what extent they were considered as the citizens of India. Harassment and extortion of money by the traffic police could be very clearly included in the garb of hate crime by public servant.

Analysis

The process of alienation by general public was not very far-fetched when one takes into account how Northeastern people were treated in India. They were perceived as an alien to what the rest of the people consider as the standard of an Indian citizen. This means that general public differentiates Northeastern people on the basis of their appearance, ethnicity, and the state they belong to; they were identified as the "others" in India. This behavior could be observed in the rest of the people of India as well as the agents of the government, i.e., the traffic police officer in this case. Lack of awareness and insensitivity makes the Northeastern people feel that they were not part of the nation India. This calls for an urgent need to sensitize as well as educate the police officers in order to recognize the existence of equal citizenship of Northeast people in India.

Case Study 4 (Chennai)

V was a mother of two living in Chennai with her husband and in-laws. They moved in the city in the early 1900s and were engaged in earning an honest living staying in the city. Both V and her husband were working, while their children were in school. V was a salesperson who goes door-to-door promoting products on the market and to launch new products in the localities. She was engaged in this line of work for a few years now and had suffered with a lot of name-calling, indecent remarks, and humiliation from the public local to Chennai. She shares her experience that it was not just once that she was subjected to identity-specific humiliation but had to go through with such indecency once in every 2–3 days. She had encountered people making indecent sexual remarks since people consider Northeast women as cheap and openly accessible women. She had been made fun of because of her accent and looks. She shares an interesting fact that till the time people assume that people like V were foreigners from China or Korea, they get respected, but as soon as they clarify that they were from Northeast part of India, they were discriminated against. V at the end of the conversation explained to the field investigator that she wants to leave the job but could not because her family's livelihood depends on hers and her husband's income combined.

Analysis

It was evident from the above case study that hate crimes not only affects the direct victim but also had other consequences that would affect an entire family. These kinds of incidents become traumatizing for the victim and affects everything around her. V in the case above feels helpless and does not think that there was a way out of this dehumanization of Northeast Indians living in Chennai. The fact that she was seen as a disrespectful woman because she belongs to a specific identity was unjust and inhuman for a woman to go through. This was an example of hate crime since she was targeted as part of a certain group and not an individual who was working for the welfare of her family. This discrimination in treatment affects her mental well-being and was gross violation of the basic human rights that every citizen of India has. It was imperative that such incidents were observed closely and in unison because these cases indicate a pattern toward the faulty perceptions that had formed in the Indian society against the Northeast Indian population.

Case Study 5 (Delhi)

This case study stood as a perfect example to the irony in *dil walon ki dilli*. A was a student studying Pol. Sci. (Hons.) from Delhi University, who migrated temporarily from her home in Tripura. She with her group of friends, also from Northeast India, decided on a weekend dinner and entertainment plan to celebrate completion of examination in their college. On a Saturday evening, all the friends dressed up for the long-awaited get-together and called a cab to reach their destination. While they were waiting for their transport, they noticed many pedestrians giving them an uncomfortable look. They tried to ignore it; however, the situation got out of hand when two police officials approached the girls and started asking questions. The police officials were patrolling at the time, and they approached the Northeastern girls when they saw those girls drawing attention of the onlookers. The officials asked inappropriate and personal questions like "what were you doing standing among so many people?" "whom were you trying to attract at this time of the evening?" "what occupation were you involved in that required you to dress like this at this time?" and many other such questions. They even passed disrespectful comments like "we know you chinky people were very modern" and "it was visible what you people were involved in." A and her friends tried to explain but to no avail. In the end, the girls were humiliated to such an extent that they had to drop the plan and leave for their respective residences instead.

This incident could be included within the garb of hate crime because of how the incident progressed with A and her friends. The events that began from the onlookers giving uncomfortable looks to the police officials questioning and commenting on the lifestyle and dignity of the Northeastern students clearly indicates a bias against them. The police official did not target them because of their gender particularly; according to the questions asked and the comments passed, it was clear that they targeted the girls because of their race and gender was ancillary in this incident.

Analysis

Hate crime was one crime where the major indicator was bias/hate toward a particular community or an affiliation; if an act does not have this basic component, it may continue to be a crime but not hate crime. In this particular case, A and her friends had been targeted because of the race they belong to and, i.e., the mongoloid race; the instance where the police identified them as chinky was a clear indication of such bias. From simple observation, it could be deducted that the police officials were stereotyping the Northeastern culture as being "modern," giving a derogatory connotation to the culture and lifestyle that they follow. Their dress code, the time of the hour in which they were outside, and the race to which they belong contributed to the police official and the people around them to assume that they were people engaged in indecent occupation. Their way of living was questioned and frowned upon because it was believed that the Northeastern girls had a westernized and so-called corrupted and indecent racial culture. This stereotyping of culture and lifestyle had been faced numerous times by the Northeast Indian women, which had resulted into them facing a lot of humiliation and discomfort. Sensitization and ethical as well as moral awareness are much needed among the people and the police officials. Proper training of the police, with regard to public relations with Northeast population of India in metro cities, would be a welcome step for combating the stereotyping behavior.

Case Study 6 (Delhi)

Being a citizen of India means it was part of your identity. It means that you belong somewhere. Northeast people of India face a major setback when it comes to identity. One of the incidents that come into light was a simple conversation that happened in the Delhi Metro Blue Line. Field investigator was travelling from the metro when he came across a Northeastern middle-aged man, P from Assam. The conversation started with the initial salutations of courtesy but soon it moved toward how P had fared in the metropolitan city of Delhi. P shared some of his experiences like the fact that he had always been called chinky, or the many times when he could not get accommodation in his yester-years because the landlords saw him as a Naxalite, or the time when his salary did not increase as comparison to his colleagues because he had retaliated against his senior for calling him "Chinese" all the time, and many more. The one thing he pointed out in the end of the conversation was that he did not bother with the name-calling or discrimination in getting an accommodation that much; what hurts him most was that even after living half of his life in India, he was not considered an Indian. He had always ignored such episodes of bias since he considered that it was understandable for an outside person to settle in another state; however, the one time when he retaliated against his senior was only because he called him "Chinese." Even after repeatedly communicating that he was Indian and that he did not like the way his senior was calling him, the practice did not stop. The feeling which rest of the people give him was discouraging in the way that he was stripped of his identity as an Indian by his own fellow citizens.

From the above case, it was clear that the experience shared by P includes various instances of bias on the basis of his race. These instances of hate crime had a source in the very fact that he was from Assam and that he looks different, like the so-called Chinese.

Analysis

Hate crime against Northeastern people of India was cruel not just because of the fact that they were harmed emotionally, mentally, or physically, it was much more than that. To devoid a person of his basic identity or to not recognize a person being part of the nation of India gives Northeastern people the feeling of insecurity and abandonment. Citizenship was the right of every citizen of India, which means the privileges of being Indian citizens were equally the right of Northeastern people. That would entail the privilege of being called Indians, protection against crimes like hate crimes, discrimination, and other such bias living in whichever part of India and equal opportunities of accommodation or work. These were basic rights of every Indian, and such preventive measures ought to be adopted in furtherance of the same, in order to provide security to the Northeastern people of India.

Case Study 7 (Hyderabad)

The most common issue that was observed in metropolitan cities was the differential treatment faced by Northeast Indian people in these areas. One such instance was reiterated by B, a Northeastern woman who lives in Pune for the reason of her job. This case was firsthand observed by one of the field investigators. On just another ordinary weekend, B and her friends ventured out for some roadside *chaat* in the daytime; our field investigator was one of them in the group. While eating *gol gappe* at the nearby food stall, a group of men in motorbikes started circling around them and were ogling at the group. They called the Northeastern people in the group, including B, names like "chinky," "squinty eyes," and "Chinese." They laughed while name-calling them, and witnessing this scenario, the public around as well as the person at the food stall joined in the laughter. After this show of so-called humor according to those men, they left the place leaving the Northeastern people of the group in humiliation. When asked about the fact as to how B felt at that moment, she responded she felt humiliation and helplessness. However, she ignored the incident and shared that it wasn't the first time that something like this had happened, where people mock her physical appearance and publicly make a spectacle out of her embarrassing situation. She felt helpless because she believes that nothing positive would come out of bringing this issue to light.

Cases like above were the most common ones when it comes to Northeast Indians in metropolitan cities. This act was where Northeast Indian people were segregated and treated differentially on the basis of their different appearance. They were caused harm in the form of annoyance and humiliation because of their different appearance, which safely puts cases like these under hate crime against these Northeastern people.

Analysis

The aforementioned case was generally treated as trivial when opinion of majority of the public comes into play. For that matter, even the Northeast Indians ignore such incidents. This was because of the simple notion that it was very common. After conversating with Northeastern people regarding this matter, it could be observed that they had learnt to accept these names; they had familiarized themselves with the identification that rest of the public gave them. This was all the more unfortunate that Northeastern people take a form of hate crime against them as a standard norm in the society. Another reason that often comes into play when we talk about reaction of the Northeastern people to such incidents was that they do not had faith in the legal machinery to redress their issue. This belief had formulated over an extended period of time with the continued experience of hate speech and hate crime against Northeast Indian people with no legal relief available to them. Provisions for sensitive and responsive legal remedies could address such incidents of name-calling and could also enable the Northeast Indian people to reinstate their faith in the legal mechanism of India.

Case Study 8 (Hyderabad)

Bullying and ragging was one of the major problems among the youth in our country. It could be because of a lot of reasons, and it mainly victimizes that section of the population which it finds different among the majority group. He was a Northeast student studying in Hyderabad. He had resided this city since 10th standard and was yet to complete his graduation. He shifted to Hyderabad with his parents for better prospects in academics and career for the family. He distinctly remembers his first day in his new school where he was teased for having "chinky eyes." Since then, it had only increased up till 11th class, after which he started to get into fights with the students who would tease him. It was only after he had created a strong and violent rapport among the students that the humiliation stopped. But because of this, he attracted a lot of negative attention among his teachers, and his academic performance dropped significantly. He shares that it was not something he wanted to do but he had no choice. During his graduation, he had faced such humiliations because of the identity. To some of those incidents, he had retaliated against, but some of them he had to let go. He iterated that there were some incidents of name-calling that included teachers and professors which gave other students the encouragement to act the same.

Analysis

It could be seen from the above example that E had been subjected to bullying and ragging because he was considered different or "other" from the rest of the population in school and during his graduation. He felt helpless in seeking help from his teachers since they encouraged this behavior as well. In order to protect himself, he felt it was better to adopt violence against the perpetrators of bullying. This chain reaction led to his own grades falling in school and being traumatized because of his identity. It could be seen from such cases that the victim loses his self-identity of a student and was only differentiated by his group identity. Due to lack of safeguard measures and adequate training among of teachers and professors in such situations, such incidents affect the mental growth and well-being in education institutions.

Case Study 9 (Mumbai)

A multipurpose one-roof destination, in simple terms called a mall, was a place where you could observe numerous instances of biasness toward Northeast Indians. One of the field investigators visited one such mall where there was beauty salon as well as a spa. On the instance of being tended to in the salon, the field investigator started inquiring about the spa and the people who work there. The employees of the salon reacted in an unusual and distasteful manner and said, "the chink employees do exactly what generally happens in a spa like that." This indirectly conveyed that they were pointing toward the indecent activities that the Northeastern employees were a part of inside the spa. When further questioned about whether they had seen something to that effect which would indicate acts of indecency or prostitution taking place inside, their answers were vague and hearsay. The most common answer that was communicated to the field investigators by the staff of the salon as well as other customers that were present at that time was that that was the obvious and common assumption considering that the Northeast Indians were so modern in their approach and lifestyle. Without seeing anything firsthand or experiencing anything concrete, Northeastern women working in the spa were branded indecent just because of the community they belong to and the lifestyle they follow.

This kind of stereotyping of Northeastern women was a classic indicator toward bias toward their particular community. They were not targeted because they were women but because they belonged to a particular community and there was a common notion that Northeast Indians were "modern" that this stereotyping was done.

Analysis

Assuming a person's character on the basis of preconceived notions that exist in the society for the community or group that the person belongs to was what was termed as stereotyping and was infamously spread across the Indian society. The above-mentioned case was the classic example of how Northeast Indians were subjected to stereotypes by the rest of the public. This stereotyping arose because of the community they belonged to. They were assumed to be "modern and open" people, portraying how this attribute was corrupted in comparison to the so-called norms and culture of the Indian society. So, unknowingly, Northeast Indians were targeted as people who were different from the Indian society. This biasness and exclusion were the product of lack of awareness and insensitivity in the general public. Dissemination of knowledge with regard to the lifestyle and culture of Northeastern people of India as well as changing attitude toward them would bring the required dignity and acceptance to this community.

Case Study 10 (Mumbai)

Mumbai was a place where people of every religion, caste, race, and gender meet and search for opportunities. It was home to varying kinds of people, and it was actually symbolic to the diverse population that India has. Northeastern people were a major section of the Mumbai population. F was a Northeastern woman who hails from Tripura but had now taken Mumbai as her home. She came to Mumbai for educational purposes and stayed back when she got placed in a good MNC. She had an accommodation which she shares with her Northeastern friend near her office. According to her account with regard to her experience in Mumbai, she seems to be grateful that the city took her in and gave education as well as a job. However, the only major setback to her experience was that she had faced certain instances which made her feel unsafe and insecure about living in Mumbai as a Northeast Indian. She and her friend, who had been together since graduation days, had faced numerous incidents where people would ogle at them because they were from Northeast India, call them names like "chinky" and "chow mien," stalk them, and stare at them uncomfortably. In a scenario where they had voiced their discontentment to such people, they were told off with comments like "you had such culture then why were you shying away from us," "why were you acting coy, we know you want the same thing," "you people were so modern, then accept the consequences also." After being commented upon in such a way, they had either changed their ways or ignored the situation altogether. They just try to reach their office or home as soon as possible whenever they encounter any such incident. F shared that although the problem of eve teasing was suffered by every woman in the city in varying degrees, as Northeast Indians, they had gone through more eve teasing incidents than any other woman.

Eve teasing was not an act that falls under hate crime per se. However, committing an act that was motivated by a person's affiliation clearly identifies such crimes as falling under the ambit of hate crimes. In such cases, hate crime becomes an aggravator to the crime that was already been done to the victim. Prejudice toward a group was something that makes all the difference.

Analysis

In the above case study, it was clear that F and her friend had been a victim of hate crime. One thing that easily distinguishes hate crime from other crimes was that the emotional disturbance or the trauma faced by the victim was far greater than the physical or visible harms that they face. This innate trauma was because of the reason that there was nothing that they could do to make things better. They could not change their identity or the race that they belong to. There was no escape from this. The only option left with them was to find a way around the situation or to ignore it altogether. This issue gives birth to the problem of people like F feeling unsafe in other parts of their own country. The stereotypes that surround Northeast people were discriminatory and unfair on a lot of levels. It snatches away their chance to reason with the injustices that they suffer since they were silenced with the preconceived understanding that the rest of the people had about them. An efficient way to best solve this problem was to strengthen measures to redress such complaints of Northeastern people and make the process Northeastern-friendly so that they report their grievances freely rather than suffering in silence.

Case Study 11 (Pune)

X, a female student from Nagaland residing in Pune, encountered a horrific incident of mental and emotional trauma, the accounts of which were shared by her sister. X lives near the camp area in Pune in a colony where other Northeastern and non-Northeastern girl students also reside. One evening after dinner, she decided to take a night walk near the area, but instead of the cold breeze of the night, she met with horrors of the dark. A man, whom she could not see or recognize due to the dark, followed her and started masturbating just behind her. She also felt something liquid, probably semen, drop to her legs too. When she started shouting and cried for help, the man escaped the scene. Next day, she went with her sister to file a complaint in the police station. The police were more willing to file her complaint and take necessary action. But the problem was that there were no means to identify who committed the crime the night before; so, the police officials were unable to provide any assistance. This was one such incident; however, numerous cases had been witnessed by Northeastern students in that area.

The above incident mentioned could be distinguished and be put under hate crime against Northeastern population in India because of the clear demarcation of the sexual offenses being committed against a specific set of people, i.e., Northeastern people of that area. The fact that Northeastern girl students were specifically targeted and harmed just because they belong to that community clearly falls under the ambit of hate crime.

Analysis

There were several indicators of "how and why" of hate crime that could be deduced from the above case study. It was pertinent to note that X was Northeastern, and similar Northeastern people were targeted in that area. The most common and natural way to distinguish these groups of people was by their physical appearance, and it was this feature of the Northeastern girl students which singles them out from the rest of the girl students. This distinguishing feature was seen as a vulnerability because of which they were attacked. There was a specific notion which conditions people to formulate a certain image against Northeastern people. The mindset could be clearly stated in the crime committed above where X was seen as someone who was easily and harmlessly approachable in a disrespectful way. Consequently, after this incident, X fears going out after sunset and mostly avoids going to secluded places alone. This incident itself was narrated by her sister, which clearly shows how uncomfortable and humiliated she felt. Also, the issue where the police officials were helpless would instill the feeling of fear and powerlessness. If there would've been fully functional helplines to address this issue there and then, the results might've been different. In the city of Delhi, there were helplines functioning to redress such issues as soon as they occur, which gives better scope of identifying and apprehending such perpetrators. A common helpline across India for addressing such issues would be a milestone.

Case Study 12 (Pune)

Corresponding to the data collected as well as according to the interactions of field investigators and researchers with Northeast Indians, there was a visible trend of migratory patterns that comes into picture. With large inflow of Northeast Indian population in the metro cities, it had caused an increase in the requirement for renting and lodging facilities by these migrated people. Similarly, M was a Northeastern man who, for reasons of employment, migrated to Pune in hopes for a better future and good living conditions. Before job hunting, he strategically planned to get a 1-bhk apartment on rent so that he could provide residency proof and related information to his future employer. However, what he faced while searching for accommodation was completely contrary to his plans. He was denied accommodation wherever he went to speculate. Even in places where he had information that there was vacant space, he was told that there was no place for him. There was also this instance where he had a telephonic conversation with a middle-aged man about an apartment for rent, but after reaching the designated place and having met the man on the telephone, he was informed that there was no vacant accommodation. He came across an agent who could arrange accommodation for M, and it was then that his confusion was cleared as to why he got rejected from every accommodation prospects. The agent informed him very bluntly that most of the people would not prefer giving an accommodation to M because he was a Northeast Indian. When he asked for a reason for the same, he was told that it was because people like M look different and were considered untrustworthy and unsafe due to their culture and the place they belong from. Finally, M did manage to find an accommodation where the landlord was Northeastern himself.

This case study clearly falls under such acts which constitute hate crimes against Northeast Indians. From the series of events, it could be observed that the sole reason as to why he wasn't given an accommodation was due to his community identity. When any act was motivated or any bias was apparent because of the group that victim belongs to, it makes such acts to fall under hate crimes.

Analysis

Accommodation problem faced by Northeast Indians in metropolitan cities was one which was most commonly observed. The end result was visibly the issue, i.e., people such as M not getting accommodation, but the real problem lies in the underlying motive or bias or prejudice that leads to such acts. How Northeast Indians were perceived was something that could not be discerned till the time such apparent cases come into light. In this case, M suffered at the hands of the landlords because of his group identity. He was "branded" to be untrustworthy and unsafe because he belongs to a specific race. This prejudice against the mongoloid race was not just limited to M since the agent was very clear as to the trend that could be commonly seen among the people of Pune. The problem here was the attitude and preconceived notions of the people against a particular race. This could only be lessened, if not totally eradicated, by proper knowledge and awareness among the people that Northeast people belong to the Indian brotherhood like every other citizen. Also, since migratory pattern was pretty much apparent in metro cities like Pune, proper accommodative facilities should be in place in order to facilitate basic amenities of living under a roof for the Northeast Indians.

Annexure 2: Interview Schedule for General Population

Demographic Profile

1. Age Group

   ☐ 18–22 years
   ☐ 23–30 years
   ☐ 31–40 years
   ☐ 40 and above

2. Gender

   ☐ Male
   ☐ Female
   ☐ Third gender

3. Occupation

   ☐ Student
   ☐ Self-employed
   ☐ Private
   ☐ Public

4. Which metro city are you currently residing in?

   ☐ Pune
   ☐ Mumbai
   ☐ New Delhi
   ☐ Bangalore
   ☐ Chennai
   ☐ Hyderabad

5. Are you aware of the term "hate crime"?

   ☐ Yes
   ☐ No

6. If yes, has anyone known to you encountered any such incident?

   ☐ Yes
   ☐ No (if no, please start answering from questions from Q. No. 16.)

7. What kind of relationship do you share with the victim?

   ☐ Neighbor
   ☐ Colleague
   ☐ Friend
   ☐ Tenants

8. What type of incident/incidents of crimes would they have majorly suffered or encountered after coming to metro city?

   ☐ Offensive and abusive language
   ☐ Coercive and threatening behavior

☐ Mediated threats
☐ Physical assault
☐ Sexual remarks
☐ Sexual assault
☐ Material and criminal damage
☐ Incitement
☐ Other (please specify.)...........................

9. Do you know the abovementioned incident/incidents are hate crimes?

☐ Yes
☐ No

10. Have you ever helped or advised them to report about the incident to any agency?

☐ Yes
☐ No (if the answer is no, please start answering the questions from Q. No. 15.)

11. If yes, to which agency was the reporting done?

☐ Police
☐ Educational organization
☐ Local councils
☐ Social enterprise
☐ Any other

12. If the incident was reported to the police, what was the reaction of the police and what was the approach adopted by them?

13. If the incident was reported to the police, was the complaint furthered by the police for investigation?

☐ Yes
☐ No

14. If yes, for how much time was the investigation conducted and what was the result?

15. If no, why they did not approach the police?

16. What do you think when you see or listen something about a person from the Northeastern states of India?

17. Have you ever felt that Northeast people are from some other country?

☐ Yes
☐ No

18. If yes, why you felt like that?

19. Have you ever been a part of hurting the sentiments of Northeast people?

☐ Yes
☐ No

20. If yes, in what form?

☐ Calling the N-E people by names like "chinky," "Nepali," etc.
☐ Comments (indirectly)
☐ Not friendly
☐ Any other (Please specify.)..............................

21. Have you ever seen anyone else hurting the sentiments of Northeast people?

☐ Yes
☐ No

22. If yes, in what form?

☐ Calling the N-E people by names like "chinky," "Nepali," etc.
☐ Comments (indirectly)
☐ Not friendly
☐ Any other (please specify)..............................

23. Do you believe that the handling of N-E people should be dealt in a different manner by the agencies?

☐ Yes
☐ No

24. If yes, why do you believe like that? (Please explain.)

25. What in your view is the major problem behind the commission of hate crimes?

☐ Geographical difference
☐ Cultural difference
☐ Physical appearance
☐ Any others (please specify)..............................

26. Do you think existing laws can cater to this problem?

☐ Yes
☐ No

27. What in your view is the possible solution to this problem?

28. Any other recommendation and comments?

Annexure 3: Interview Schedule for Northeast Population

Demographic Profile

1. Age Group

☐ 18–22 years
☐ 23–30 years

- ☐ 31–40 years
- ☐ 41 and above

2. Gender

- ☐ Male
- ☐ Female
- ☐ Third gender

3. Occupation

- ☐ Student
- ☐ Self-employed
- ☐ Private
- ☐ Public

4. Which metro city are you currently residing in?

- ☐ Pune
- ☐ Mumbai
- ☐ New Delhi
- ☐ Bangalore
- ☐ Chennai
- ☐ Hyderabad

5. Which part of N-E region do you belong from?

- ☐ Assam
- ☐ Manipur
- ☐ Sikkim
- ☐ Nagaland
- ☐ Meghalaya
- ☐ Arunachal Pradesh
- ☐ Mizoram
- ☐ Tripura

6. Which tribe do you belong to? (Please specify.)

7. Do you face a regional divide after shifting to the metro city?

- ☐ Yes
- ☐ No

8. If yes, what could be the reason for the same? (Can select more than one as well?)

- ☐ Geographical difference
- ☐ Cultural difference
- ☐ Physical appearance
- ☐ Other (please specify)…………………………

9. Are you aware of the term “hate crime”?

☐ Yes
☐ No

10. If yes, have you encountered any such incident?

☐ Yes
☐ No

11. Have you encountered such hate crime incidents happening with anyone else?

☐ Yes
☐ No

12. What type of incident/incidents of crime have you majorly suffered or addressed after coming to the metro city?

☐ Offensive and abusive language
☐ Coercive and threatening behavior
☐ Mediated threats
☐ Physical assault
☐ Sexual remarks
☐ Sexual assault
☐ Material and criminal damage
☐ Incitement
☐ Other (please specify)..........................

13. Do you know the abovementioned incident/incidents are hate crimes?

☐ Yes
☐ No

14. Have you faced violence or attack being a person from Northeastern states?

☐ Yes
☐ No

15. If yes, what was your mental status and physical status after facing such violence or attack? (Please describe.)

16. When did you first experience an incident of hate crime with yourself? Please elaborate.

17. How frequently have you been victimized?

☐ Very often
☐ Often
☐ Rarely
☐ Very rarely

18. Did you report the incident to any agency?

☐ Yes
☐ No (if the answer is no, please start answering the questions from Q. No. 24)

19. Which agency did you report to?

☐ Police
☐ Educational organization
☐ Local councils
☐ Social enterprise
☐ Any other

20. If you approached the police, how did the police personnel treat you being a victim of hate crime?

☐ Refused to file a complaint or FIR
☐ Demanding money to do their duties
☐ Not considered as victim
☐ Not considered hate crime or racial abuse as crime
☐ Blaming us for being a person from a Northeastern state

21. What was the reaction of the police and what was the approach adopted by the police?

22. Was your complaint furthered by the police for investigation?

☐ Yes
☐ No

23. If yes, for how much time was the investigation conducted and what was the result?

24. If no, why did you not approach the police?

25. Are you aware of any other agency that redresses the issue of hate crime?

☐ Yes
☐ No

26. If yes, did you approach any of them and what was your experience with that agency?

27. Have you ever really felt bad or cried for being abused racially?

☐ Yes
☐ No

28. If yes, how often have you really felt bad or cried for being abused racially?

☐ Very often
☐ Often
☐ Rarely
☐ Very rarely

29. How do your friends or colleagues treat you being a person from a Northeastern state?

☐ Like any other friends or colleagues
☐ Differentiate racially or treat like a person from another country
☐ Very protective being minority

30. How does your immediate boss treat you for being a person from a Northeastern state (applicable only for working person)?

☐ Like any other friends or colleagues
☐ Differentiate racially or treat like person from another country
☐ Very protective being minority

31. Do you discuss about hate crime with family, relative, or friends?

☐ Yes (if yes, answer Q. No. 32)
☐ No (if no, answer Q. No. 33)

32. If yes, what was their reaction?

33. If no, why you don't discuss?

34. What in your view is the major problem behind the commission of hate crimes?

35. Who are all the possible perpetrators? (Can select more than one as well?)

☐ Landlord
☐ Neighbors
☐ Friends/acquaintances
☐ People at workplace
☐ People at school
☐ Stranger/s
☐ Police officer/s
☐ Any other (please specify)...

36. Could you describe the attitude of the perpetrators of hate crime?

37. Are you afraid of living in the current metro city where you are living?

☐ Yes
☐ No

38. Are you afraid or worried of being subject to verbal abuse, physical attack, vandalism, property damage, or theft because of your identity of being a person from a NE state of India?

☐ Yes
☐ No

39. If yes, how often are you afraid or worried?

- ☐ Very often
- ☐ Often
- ☐ Rarely
- ☐ Very rarely

40. What was the effect on yourself after you became a victim of the hate crime?

- ☐ Avoided going out at night
- ☐ Avoid going to place/s where you experienced the hate crime
- ☐ Started going out at certain time of the day, which you considered to be safe
- ☐ Changed your schedule
- ☐ Stopped going out alone
- ☐ Retaliated against it
- ☐ Avoided the situation
- ☐ Any other

41. Are you aware of the following laws which are in existence to prevent hate crimes?

    (a) Section 153A of the Indian Penal Code
    (b) Schedule Castes and Tribes (Prevention of Atrocities) Act, 1989
    (c) Not aware

42. If you are aware, do you think these existing laws can cater to this problem?

43. What in your view is the possible solution to this problem?

44. Are you aware about the Bezbaruah committee recommendations?

- ☐ Yes
- ☐ No

45. If yes, do you think that the successful implementation of the recommendations given by the Bezbaruah committee will solve the problem faced by the people from Northeast India?

- ☐ Yes
- ☐ No

46. Any other recommendation and comments?

Annexure 4: Informed Consent Form for the General Population

You are invited to be in a research study of **Hate Crimes: Prejudices and Violence Faced by People from Northeastern States and Measures to Counter – An Empirical Study (A Study of Metro Cities in India.** The project director and principal investigator of this research study is Prof. (Dr.) G S Bajpai, Professor (Criminology and Criminal Justice) and The Registrar, National Law University, Delhi, and this research study is funded by the ***Indian Council of Social Science Research, Government of India, New Delhi.*** The purpose of this research project is to analyze the prejudices and violence faced by people from the Northeastern states and measures to counter it. You were selected as a possible participant according to the purpose of our research study which is about people from the Northeastern states in India, but we are also collecting data from general population views about the prejudices and violence faced by people from the Northeastern states.

Your participation in this research study is purely on the voluntary basis only. If you decide to participate in this research study, you will be asked to participate in an interview schedule which will take you approximately 10–15 min. You have all rights to withdraw from participating in the research study at any time or leave blank any of the questions you don't wish to answer. If you withdraw from participating at any time or don't answer any question, you will not be penalized.

The survey questions will be about your day-to-day experience in the metro cities of India being a person from Northeastern India and problems you have encountered being a person from Northeastern India.

Information collected through this exercise shall be kept confidential and shall be used for academic purposes only. To help protect your confidentiality and maintain anonymity, the data collection will not involve any collection of personal information that will personally identify you.

If you have any questions about the research study, please contact our field coordinator.

By signing this consent form, you indicate that you have read the above information and agree voluntarily to participate in the research study.

I agree to participate in **Hate Crimes: Prejudices and Violence Faced by People from Northeastern States and Measures to Counter – An Empirical Study (A Study of Metro Cities in India,** as set out above. I understand that the data collected from my participation will be used for academic/research purpose only, and I consent for it to be used in that manner.

Name (bold letters)……………………………….
Participant's signature ……………………………. Date…………………

Annexure 5: Informed Consent Form for Northeast Population

You are invited to be in a research study of **Hate Crimes: Prejudices and Violence Faced by People from Northeastern States and Measures to Counter – An Empirical Study (A Study of Metro Cities in India.** The project director and principal investigator of this research study is Prof. (Dr.) G S Bajpai, Professor (Criminology and Criminal Justice) and The Registrar, National Law University, Delhi, and this research study is funded by the **Indian Council of Social Science Research, Government of India, New Delhi.** The purpose of this research project is to analyze the prejudices and violence faced by people from Northeastern states and measures to counter it. You were selected as a possible participant according to the purpose of our research study which is about people from the Northeastern states in India.

Your participation in this research study is purely on the voluntary basis only. If you decide to participate in this research study, you will be asked to participate in an interview schedule which will take you approximately 10–15 min. You have all rights to withdraw from participating in the research study at any time or leave blank any of the questions you don't wish to answer. If you withdraw from participating at any time or don't answer any question, you will not be penalized.

The survey questions will be about your day-to-day experience in the metro cities of India being a person from Northeastern India and problems you have encountered being a person from Northeastern India.

Information collected through this exercise shall be kept confidential and shall be used for academic purposes only. To help protect your confidentiality and maintain anonymity, the data collection will not involve any collection of personal information that will personally identify you.

If you have any questions about the research study, please contact our field coordinator.

By signing this consent form, you indicate that you have read the above information and agree voluntarily to participate in the research study.

I agree to participate in **Hate Crimes: Prejudices and Violence Faced by People from Northeastern States and Measures to Counter – An Empirical Study (A Study of Metro Cities in India,** as set out above. I understand that the data collected from my participation will be used for academic/research purposes only, and I consent for it to be used in that manner.

Name (bold letters)……………………………………..
Participant's signature ……………………………… Date…………………

Annexure 6: Electronic Consent

ELECTRONIC CONSENT: Please select your choice below.

Clicking on the "agree" button below indicates that:

- You have read the above information.
- You voluntarily agree to participate.
- You are at least 18 years of age.

If you do not wish to participate in the research study, please decline participation by clicking on the "disagree" button.

Bibliography

Books

Baruah, S. (2007). *Durable disorder: Understanding the politics of North-East India*. Oxford India.
Bhaumik, S. (2005). *Troubled periphery: The crisis of India's North-East*. Sage Publications India.
Gerstenfeld, P. B. (2011). *Hate crimes: Causes, controls and controversies*. Sage.
Hazarika, S. (1994). *Strangers of the mist: Tales of war and peace from India's North-East Viking*. Penguin Books India.
Hindpal Singh Bhui, D. S. (2009). *Race and criminal justice*. Sage.
Leonard, C. R. (2014). *Beyond hate: White power and popular culture*. Dorset Press.
McDuie-Ra, D. (2012). *North-East migrants in Delhi race, refuge and retail*. Amsterdam University Press.
Mukhim, P. (2006). Where is the North-East? In G. Sen (Ed.), *When the sun rises when shadows fall: The North-East*. Oxford University Press.
Singh , B. P. (1987). *The problem of change: A study of Northeast India*. Oxford University Press.
Thakur, D. (2009). *Law and administration*. Deep and Deep Publications Ltd.
Wolfe, Z. J. (2014). *Hate crimes law*. Thomson Reuters.

Journal Articles

Aamreshwaran, D. N. (2017). Problems of North-East People in metro cities of India: Need of human values of happy and healthy life. *International Journal of Education and Multidisciplinary Studies*, 2013–2018.
Angel, T. L. (1995). A people distinct from others: Race and identity in federal Indian Law and the Hispanic classifications in OMB directive no. 15. *Texas Tech Law Review, 26*(4), 1219–1274.
Bajpai, G. S., & Pal, G. (2018). Exigency for law on hate crime against racial minorities: A comparative study with special reference to North-East people in India. *MNLU Contemporary Law Review, 2*(2), 283–293.
Baruah, S. (2005). A new politics of race: India and its North-East. *India International Centre Quarterly, 32*(2), 163–176.
Baruah, S. (2007a). *Durable disorder: Understanding the politics of North-East India*. Oxford India.

G. S. Bajpai et al., *Hate Crime in India*,
https://doi.org/10.1007/978-3-031-30522-1

Baruah, S. (2007b). *Postfrontier blues: Toward a new policy framework for North-East India*. East-West Center Washington.

Bhattarai, B. (2015). Reconsider India's North-East in national curriculum. *American International Journal of Research in Humanities, Arts and Social Sciences*, 132–134.

Bhaumik, S. (2005). *Troubled periphery: The crisis of India's North-East*. Sage Publishing India.

Bijukumar, V. (2013, July). Social exclusion and ethnicity in Northeast India. *The NEHU Journal, 11*(2), 19–35.

Bora, P. (2019). The problem without a name: Comments on cultural difference (racism) in India. *South Asia: Journal of South Asian Studies, 42*(5), 845–860.

Chakraborti, N., & Garland, J. (2012). Reconceptualising hate crime victimization through the lens of vulnerability and 'difference'. *Theoretical Criminology, 16*(4), 499–514.

Debbarma, R. K. (2016). How not to fight discrimination in India desire, difference and the North-East. *Economic and Political Weekly, LI, 26–27*, 25–29.

Dev, R. (2004, October 23–24). Human rights, relativism and minorities in North-East India. *Economic and Political Weekly, 39*(43), 4747–4752.

Goregenli, P. K. (2011). Who is guilty? Undergraduate students' attitude towards hate crimes based on sexual orientation. *International Journal of Arts and Science of*, 253–264.

Hazarika, S. (1994). *Strangers of the mist: Tales of war and peace from India's North-East Viking*. Penguin Books India.

Hurd, H. M. (2001, March). Why liberals should hate "hate crime legislation". *Law and Philosophy, 20*(2), 215–232.

Jain, N. (2016a, September). North-East India's multi-ethnicities: Dominant issues and problems. *International Journal of Humanities & Social Science Studies, 3*(2), 275–285.

Jain, N. (2016b). North-East India's Multiple Ethnicities: Dominant Issues and Problems. *International Journal of Humanities and Social Science Studies*, 275–285.

Kumar, M. S., & Zou, D. V. (2011). North-East, mapping a colonial borderland: Objectifying the geo-body of India's. *The Journal of Asian Studies, 70*(1), 141–170.

Lyons, C. J. (2006). Stigma or sympathy? Attributions of fault to hate crimes and offenders. *Social Psychology Quarterly, 69*, 39–59.

Madhab, J. (1999, February 6–12). North-East: Crisis of identity, security and underdevelopment. *Economic and Political Weekly, 34*(6), 320–322.

Mal, K. V. (2015). Understanding language & culture: Bridging the gap between Delhi city & North-East students. *DU Journal of Undergraduate Reserach and Innovation, 1*(2), 144–153.

McDuie-Ra, D. (2012a). Beyond the 'Exclusionary City': North-east migrants in neo-liberal Delhi. *Urban Studies, 50*(8), 1625–1640.

McDuie-Ra, D. (2012b). *North-East migrants in Delhi: Race, refuge and retail*. Amsterdam University Press.

McDuie-Ra, D. (2012c). The 'North-East' map of Delhi. *Economic and Political Weekly, 47*(30), 69–77.

McDuie-Ra, D. (2013). Leaving the North-East borderland: Placemaking & the inward pull of citizenship in India. *Eurasia Border Review*, 1–17.

McDuie-Ra, D. (2015a). 'Is India Racist?' Murder, migration and Mary Kom. *Journal of South Asian Studies, 38*(2), 304–319.

McDuie-Ra, D. (2015b). Adjacent identities in Northeast India. *Asian Ethnicity*, 400–413.

Mukhim, P. (2006). Where is the Northeast? In G. Sen (Ed.), *When the sun rises when shadows fall: The Northeast*. Oxford University Press.

Murakami, T. K. (2004). Hate crimes. *Georgeton Journal of Gender and the Law, 5*(1), 63–76.

Nghaite, T. (2014). Nido Taniam and the fraught question of racism in India. *Economic and Political Weekly, 49*(11), 15–17.

Punathil, S., & Sitlhou, H. (2017, April), Research in progress: Racial Discrimination and Violence against Northeasterners and the Bezbaruah Committee Report, 2014. *Explorations, 1*(1), 90–101.

Raj, S. (2016, December 1), From marginalisation to stereotypes – 'North-East India' in Indian media: Evidences from focus group discussions in Manipur. *Journal of North-East India Studies, 6*(2), 70–79.
Ramesh, B. P. (2012, June 2), Strangers in their own land: Migrants from North-East in Delhi. *Economic and Political Weekly, 47*(22), 35–40.
Ramesh, J. (2005). *North-East India in a new Asia*. Seminar.
Remesh, B. P. (2012, June 2), Strangers in their own land: Migrants from the North-East in Delhi. *Economic and Political Weekly, 47*(22), 35–40.
Samson, K. (2017), North-East and Chinky: Countenances of racism in India. *The Journal of Development Practice , 3*.
Samuel, J. (1993, January 16–23), Language and nationality in North-East India. *Economic and Political Weekly, 28*(3), 91–92.
Singh, B. P. (1987). *The problem of change: A study of Northeast India*. Oxford University Press.
Teltumbde, A. (2014). On the murder of Nido Taniam. *Economic & Political Weekly, 49*(11).
Th, S. (2014). Racial Discrimination in India: (Special reference to racial attacks on people of North-East in Delhi). *International Journal of Physical and Social Sciences, 4*(10), 478–500.
Thakur, D. (2009). *Law and administration*. Deep and Deep Publications Ltd.
Thounaojam, S. (2012, August 11), A preface to racial discourse in India: North-East and mainland. *Economic and Political Weekly, 47*(32), 10–13.
Waldo, C. (2018). So what's hate crime anyway? Young adults' perception of hate crimes, victims and perpetrators. *Law and Human Behavior, 20*(2), 113–129.

Reports

Barkataki, T. (2017), Discrimination and the rising of North-East- A long way to go. In *(Re) envisaging India's North-East: Ethnicity, identity, culture and literature.*
Berbaruah, M. (2014). *Report of the committee under the Chairmanship of Shri M.P. Bezbaruah to look into the concerns of the people of North-East living in other parts of the country*. Government of India.
Chauhan, J. B. (2017). *Hate speech*. Law Commission of India.
Fedrick, L. (2012). *Racialisation and caste in India* (Working Paper). CERS.
Finn, P., & McNeil, T. (1987). *The response of the criminal justice system to bias crimes: An exploratory review*. National Institute of Justice/ABT Associates Inc.
OSCE. (2014). *Prosecuting hate crimes*. OSCE ODIHR.
Reuter, N. (2009). *Hate crimes: A practical guide*. OSCE ODIHR.
The AICC Center for North-East Relations. (2015). *Five years report: The challenges faced by North-East communities in metro cities (2011–2015)*. All India Christian Council.

Case Law

Brown v. Board of Education of Topeka, 347 U.S. 483 (US Supreme Court May 17, 1954).
In Re Joshua H., 13 Cal.App.4th 1734 (Court of Appeal of California, Sixth District March 8, 1993).
Wisconsin v. Mitchell, 508 U.S. 476 (US Supreme Court 1993).

Web Resources

Bhat, M. A. (2018, August 14). *Assault on North-East Indians: This racism must end, and here's how you can help*. Retrieved October, 2019, from https://www.hindustantimes.com/analysis/mob-lynching-should-be-categorised-as-a-class-of-hate-crimes/story-0NvzhshQfKg6h2dhm3NXRM.html

Crown Prosecution Service. (2017). *Public statement on prosecuting racist and religious hate crime*. Retrieved from https://www.cps.gov.uk

Federal Bureau of Investigation. (2016). *Hate crime statistic*. FBI: Uniform Crime Reporting. Retrieved from https://www.ucr.fbi.gov/hate-crime

Hazara, I. (2014, February 10). *Racism, our dirty secret*. Retrieved from https://www.timesofindia.indiatimes.com/edit-page/Racism-our-dirty-secret/articleshow/30121070.cms

Hazarika, S. (2017, August 11). Discrimination, being North-Eastern and 'Indian-ness'. *Hindustan Times*. Retrieved from https://www.hindustantimes.com/analysis/discrimination-being-north-eastern-and-indian-ness/story-s8Y33kar75WFkH4CdGkV8H.html

Hindes, D. (2005, April 17), *Defining racism*. Daniel Hindes. Retrieved from https://www.danielhindes.com/blog/2005/04/17/defining-racism/

Jilangamba, Y. (2016, July 12), *Let's stop pretending there's no racism in India*. Retrieved from https://www.thehindu.com/opinion/op-ed/lets-stop-pretending-theres-no-racism-in-india/article3466554.ece

Khadka, M. (2018, March 19), *How do Indians view people from the Northeast part of India? How are these opinions different from how other Indians are viewed?* Retrieved from https://www.quora.com/How-do-Indians-view-people-from-the-Northeast-part-of-India-How-arc-these-opinions-different-from-how-other-Indians-are-viewed

Mackinnon, B. (2014). *Ethics- Theory and contemporary issues*. Cengage Learning.

National Institute of Justice. (2010, December 21). *Overview of hate crime*. National Institute of Justice. Retrieved from https://www.nij.ojp.gov/topics/articles/overview-hate-crime

O'Neill, A. (2017, October 17). *Hate crime, England and Wales, 2016/17*. Retrieved from https://www.assets.publishing.service.gov.uk/government/uploads/system/uploads/attachment_data/file/652136/hate-crime-1617-hosb1717.pdf

OSCE ODIHR. (2016, November 16). *What is hate crime*. Hate Crime Reporting. Retrieved from https://www.hatecrime.osce.org/what-hate-crime

S, L. P. (2017, November 27). *Assault on Northeast Indians: This racism must end, and here's how you can help*. The Better India. Retrieved from https://www.thebetterindia.com/122478/assault-northeast-indians-racism-must-end-heres-can-help/

Sharma, A. (2012, June 3). North-East racial slur could get you jailed for five years. *India Today*. Retrieved from https://www.indiatoday.in/india/north/story/north-east-racial-slur-home-ministry-sc-st-act-jail-term-104281-2012-06-03

The United States Department of Justice. (2019, March 7). *Hate Crime Laws*, The United States Department of Justice, Retrieved from https://www.justice.gov/crt/hate-crime-laws

Miscellaneous

Ahmad, N. (2017, January). Racism in India: Equality constitutionalism and lego-institutional response. *Comparitive Law Prof Blog*.

Bhanjdeo, A. M. (2015). India and Its North-East exception: From frontier to forefront. *Senior Projects Spring 2015*. Bard College.

Baruah, S. (2007). *Postfrontier blues: Toward a new policy framework for North-East India*. East-West Center Washington.

Ramesh, J. (2005). *Northeast India in a new Asia*. Seminar.

Index

G. S. Bajpai et al., *Hate Crime in India*,
https://doi.org/10.1007/978-3-031-30522-1

MIX
Papier aus verantwortungsvollen Quellen
Paper from responsible sources
FSC® C105338

If you have any concerns about our products,
you can contact us on
ProductSafety@springernature.com

In case Publisher is established outside the EU,
the EU authorized representative is:
Springer Nature Customer Service Center GmbH
Europaplatz 3, 69115 Heidelberg, Germany

Printed by Libri Plureos GmbH
in Hamburg, Germany